WILLIAM BLAKE'S WATER-COLOURS

ILLUSTRATING THE POEMS OF THOMAS GRAY

with an Introduction and Commentary by

Sir Geoffrey Keynes

Published by J. Philip O'Hara, Inc., Chicago

in association with Trianon Press, Paris

1972

William Blake

Drawn by John Flaxman

P O E M S.

BY

MR. GRAY.

Drawings
by

William Blake

A NEW EDITION.

LONDON:

PRINTED FOR J. MURRAY, (No. 32.) FLEET-
STREET.

MDCCLXXXX.

The first complete edition of William Blake's
Water-colour Designs for the Poems of Thomas Gray
was published in June 1972 by the Trianon Press
Château de Boissia, Clairvaux, Jura, France
and 125 avenue du Maine, Paris 14ᵉ
This edition was coloured by hand
and strictly limited to 518 numbered copies

The present edition, entitled William Blake's
Water-colours Illustrating the Poems of Thomas Gray
is published by J. Philip O'Hara, Inc.
20 East Huron, Chicago 60611
in association with Trianon Press, Paris
Published simultaneously in Canada by
Van Nostrand Reinhold Ltd., Scarborough, Ontario

The eight-colour offset plates were made by
Victor-Michel, Paris and Rossi, Lyon
and printed by the Imprimerie Moderne du Lion, Paris
under the supervision of Fernand Chenot
and Arnold Fawcus who designed and produced the book

The text was composed in Monotype Bembo
and printed by the Imprimerie Darantiere, Dijon
The binding was by Engel, Malakoff

CONTENTS

To Julie

In gratitude for her help

G.L.K. & A.D.F.

ACKNOWLEDGEMENTS

It is difficult to understand why, approximately 175 years after they were commissioned by Blake's friend, John Flaxman, this astonishing series of water-colours have only recently emerged and received the recognition that they so justly merit.

A combination of circumstances seems to have conspired, even in Blake's lifetime, to keep them out of view. We know from a letter written in 1805 by their first owner, Ann Flaxman, to whom Blake dedicated the series, that she was not in the habit of showing them to all and sundry. Referring to the Rev. Joseph Thomas, Rector of Epsom, she wrote to her husband: '[He] wishes as a great favor the loan of *Blake's Gray* to amuse himself with promising that it shall not go from his chamber or be wantonly shewn to anybody'. Such discretion was probably thought necessary since Blake had characteristically included elements of his own political protest, such as his republican and anti-war views, which might have got him into trouble.

Blake had two brushes with the law, the first, some time between 1779-1782, when he and his friends, Stothard and Ogleby, were arrested as spies while on a sketching trip up the Medway, and the second in 1804, the year before the letter quoted above was written, when he was subjected to the ordeal of a trial for 'sedition' at Chichester on the accusation of two soldiers who claimed Blake had 'uttered seditious and treasonable expressions such as D..n the King d..n all his subjects d..n his soldiery they are all slaves'. Fortunately the outcome was a happy one in both cases. In the first, members of the Royal Academy identified the trio as harmless artists; in the second, the evidence of neighbours and the support of the local gentry cleared Blake of all charges. If one bears in mind that the sentence for treason or sedition was death, it is not surprising that Blake's friends should have been careful about showing any of his drawings which might be given a revolutionary interpretation.

Sir Geoffrey Keynes, the Chairman of the William Blake Trust, in his authoritative Introduction discusses the origins of the designs and traces their history from their 'disappearance' for over fifty years to their recent acquisition by Mr. Paul Mellon, an Associate Trustee of the Blake Trust.

To Mr. Mellon we owe a very great debt of gratitude. Soon after acquiring these marvellous water-colours he most generously parted with them for a prolonged period, four years, so that they could be reproduced in our workshops in Paris, and has, by a munificent gift, made possible their recent publication in the series of the

Blake Trust hand-coloured facsimiles. He has also enabled us in the present volume to include more colour plates than had originally been intended. On the completion of the facsimile he generously allowed the designs to be shown to the public for the first time at an exhibition arranged by the Blake Trust at the Tate Gallery, London in December 1971 and the following spring at an exhibition at the Yale Art Gallery under the aegis of the Paul Mellon Center for British Art and British Studies.

The present publication was planned as an introductory study of Blake's remarkable designs and was first published as a handbook to accompany the exhibitions referred to above.

To Sir Geoffrey Keynes I am grateful as always for his unstinting advice and help at every stage of the production of this volume and for writing the Introduction and the Commentary.

I am indebted, too, to the Trustees of the William Blake Trust for their guidance in solving various problems as they arose and particularly to Peter du Sautoy who has generously given me the benefit of his great experience in every aspect of publishing.

I wish also to thank Mr. Herbert Bailey for his assistance, and Mrs. Irene Tayler who kindly lent us proofs before publication of her book, *Blake's Illustrations to the Poems of Gray*, Princeton University Press 1971, to which we refer the reader for a more detailed study of the designs in this series.

ARNOLD FAWCUS

LIST OF POEMS AND ILLUSTRATIONS
Concordance of Blake's handwritten titles

Blake's manuscript titles are given in italics, and the verses taken from Gray's lines are quoted exactly as Blake wrote them, including spelling and punctuation. On each page of Gray's verses, with four exceptions, Blake indicated the passage he intended to illustrate by marking the first line with a small pencil cross; this is given in smaller type in roman. The punctuation in these lines has been retained and dialogue is indicated by double quotation marks. Blake also numbered the illustrations of each poem separately in the top left- or right- hand corner to correspond with the numbers in his lists of titles; these numbers are referred to as ms. no. throughout the book. To assist identification, the page number of Gray's text in the 1790 edition is given, and for easier reference the 116 designs have also been allotted consecutive numbers.

Titles and lines illustrated	Ms. no. (Blake)	Page no. (Gray)	Design no. (in sequence)	Page no. (Commentary)
The Pindaric Genius recieving his Lyre [Title-page for the whole series]	[1]	[precedes I]	I	41
Gray writing his Poems [List of titles for 'Ode on the Spring']	2	[precedes I]	2	41
ODE ON THE SPRING				
The Purple Year awaking from the Roots of Nature *& The Hours suckling their Flowery Infants* 'And wake the purple year!'	3	43	3	41
'With me the Muse shall sit & think *At ease reclind in rustic state'* 'With me the Muse shall sit, and think'	4	44	4	42
'Brush'd by the hand of rough Mischance *Or chilld by Age'* 'Brush'd by the hand of rough Mischance'	5	45	5	42
Summer Flies reproaching the Poet 'Thy joys no glitt'ring female meets,'	6	46	6	42
ODE ON THE DEATH OF A FAVOURITE CAT **DROWNED IN A TUB OF GOLD FISHES**				
'Midst the tide *Two Angel forms were seen to glide'* [Title-page]	I	47	7	43
'Demurest of the Tabby kind' [List of titles]	2	48	8	44

xix

Introduction

WILLIAM BLAKE was an assiduous reader of the English poets from an early period of his life, and there can be no doubt that as a youth he was familiar with the poems of Thomas Gray. It is clear that the poem which most caught his fancy was 'The Bard', containing all the elements of drama, legend, imagination and prophetic utterance likely to be found most appealing by the young poet and artist. The image of the Welsh poet-prophet was described by Gray in the lines:

> Robed in the sable garb of woe,
> With haggard eyes the Poet stood;
> (Loose his beard, and hoary hair
> Stream'd, like a meteor, to the troubled air;)
> And with a master's hand, and prophet's fire,
> Struck the deep sorrows of his lyre.

Gray's description is said to have been derived from a well known picture by Raphael in the Pitti Gallery at Florence representing the Deity in Ezekiel's Vision, which was perhaps the prototype of all the ancient bearded men seen so often in Blake's pictures and heard intoning so many prophetic utterances in his poems. It is possible that Blake had seen an engraving after Raphael's painting, though his own conception was derived from Gray's lines rather than from the dignified figure supported by cherubs conceived by Raphael. Blake's earliest 'old man' figure, copied when he was but sixteen years old from Michelangelo's picture of the Crucifixion of St. Peter and later named 'Joseph of Arimathea', was a milder conception, soon to be supplanted in Blake's mind by Gray's grander image.

Blake first exhibited a water-colour drawing at the Royal Academy in 1780, the subject being 'The Death of Earl Godwin', but this was a very minor work. In 1784 he aimed much higher, shewing two water-colours, larger and more imaginative, entitled 'A breach in a city, the morning after a battle' and 'War unchain'd by an angel, Fire, Pestilence and Famine following'. In 1785 he exhibited five more, four being incidents in the story of Joseph and his Brethren, and the fifth (no. 607 in the catalogue) being 'The Bard, from Gray'. This was to be seen in the 'Exhibition Room of Sculpture and Drawings' between 'The Prophet Elijah bringing to the widow her recovered child', painted by 'a young Lady', and 'The Birth of Adonis from Ovid' by J.C. Huck. Not far from it were three sculptures by John Flaxman and 'The Death of Sir Philip Sidney' by the painter, Thomas Stothard, both artists being close friends of Blake's early years. Blake's drawing is not now known to be extant, but, as was so characteristic of him, the image of the Bard persisted in his mind's eye. It appeared again in one of the tiny copper plates of *All Religions are One*, a small didactic work executed in 1788, and yet again in 1789 as part of the decoration in the *Songs of Innocence* for the poem 'The Voice of the Ancient Bard'. In the later combined volume, *Songs of Innocence and of Experience*, Blake renumbered the plate and placed it at the end of *Songs of Experience*. The subject was later greatly enlarged in the dark, though fine, tempera painting of 'The Bard, from Gray', now in the Tate Gallery. Under Number IV in the *Descriptive Catalogue* written for his exhibition of 1809 Blake wrote of the subject:

> King Edward and his Queen Elenor are prostrated, with their horses, at the foot of a rock on which the Bard stands; prostrated by the terrors of his harp on the margin of the river Conway, whose waves bear up a corse of a slaughtered bard at the foot of the rock. The armies of Edward are seen winding among the mountains. . . Mortimer and Gloucester lie spell bound behind their king.

In a previous paragraph Blake claimed that painting must be allowed an equality with poetry and music in 'its own proper sphere of invention and visionary conception'. Indeed, this last use of the Bard theme from Gray's poem had been preceded by an extraordinary explosion of 'invention and visionary conceptions' in the form of hundreds of water-colour designs illustrating the works of two poets, Young and Gray. Blake also executed a large pencil sketch, now in the Philadelphia Museum, for the 'Bard' tempera painting.

It has often been pointed out that Blake devoted his pictorial art almost entirely to the illustration of written works, notably the Bible and the poems of Milton, so that he was what is commonly called a 'literary artist', a term sometimes used in a derogatory sense. This is, however, in no way a belittlement of Blake's renown as an artist. He did, in fact, uniquely combine the arts of painting and poetry, the chief manifestation of this being seen in his series of Illuminated Books beginning with *Songs of Innocence*, 1789, and ending with *Jerusalem*, 1818. He regarded the faculty of imagination as a divine gift serving to equate Man with God, and imagination could obviously be most fruitfully used in this combination of the arts. There was no reason for limiting his illustrations to his own poetry. Other poets could furnish ideas for his imagination to feed on, and one of the most startling results of this was the production of 537 water-colour designs for the *Night Thoughts* of Edward Young. The records make it plain that this task was not begun spontaneously, but was commissioned by the London bookseller and publisher, Richard Edwards. Nevertheless Blake accepted it with enthusiasm. He completed his work within two years and had engraved forty-three of the designs on large copper plates for publication in 1797. It was intended that further parts containing a total of two hundred plates should be engraved, but circumstances, political and social, discouraged any further production and no more were done. Blake must have been deeply disappointed at receiving no further reward for this great enterprise, though clearly his efforts had been admired by at least one faithful friend and by this friend's wife. Mrs. Ann Flaxman, commonly known as 'Nancy', had been writing enthusiastically to an acquaintance in March 1796 about Blake's designs for Young, and in another letter, undated though certainly written early in November 1797[1], she wrote of Blake as 'one who has sung his wood-notes wild—of a strong and singular Imagination he has treated his Poet most Poetically—Flaxman has employ'd him to Illuminate the works of Gray for my Library'. Dr. Mary R. Woodworth's recent discovery of this letter has settled the question, long undetermined, of when and why Blake began to make the 116 pages of water-colour designs for Gray's poems, carrying on with hardly a pause the inspiration derived from Young in a similar manner and with equal success.

Blake's method of working was similar to that which he had used for Young. Taking the 1790 edition of *Gray's Poems* (published by J. Murray, No. 31 Fleet-Street), he kept the title-page, but discarded thirty-two pages of preliminary matter (the publisher's 'Advertisement' and 'A Short Account of Gray's Life and Writings') and the ten leaves of Notes by Gray at the end. He had certainly read these and some references will be made to them in the following Commentary. The book also contained seven commonplace engraved plates, four having been specially made for this edition, but Blake owed nothing to any of these. It remained for him to take the body of the book with the poems and all the fly-titles except the one for the 'Epitaph', that is pages 43-142, 145-158, and these he used for his 116 illustrations. Trimming off the margins, he inlaid each page in a rectangular window cut out off-centre from a large sheet of Whatman drawing paper dated 1794 in the water-mark, perhaps part of the stock which had been provided by Edwards for the work on Young. Most pages of the text were printed on both sides; but by using the blank versos of fly-titles or the blank page resulting when the poem ended on a recto, Blake was enabled to write a list of the subjects illustrated in the poem following. These might give a quotation from the poem itself or a title invented by Blake. The number of each title corresponds to a handwritten pagination on the left- or right-hand top corner of the appropriate page, recto or verso. On every page of

[1] British Museum, Add. MS 39790, ff. 3-4. See the article by Dr. Mary K. Woodworth of Bryn Mawr College in *Notes & Queries*, ccxv, 1970, pp. 312-13.

verse, with four exceptions, Blake has indicated with an X the line or lines illustrated. There are three pages without either text or list: two panels following 'The Fatal Sisters' and 'The Triumphs of Owen' have been left blank; a third, the last page of the 'Elegy', carries Blake's manuscript dedication to Ann Flaxman.

Blake had prefaced his work on the verso of the title-page with the lines:

> Around the Springs of Gray my wild root weaves.
> Traveller repose & Dream among my leaves.

This was impersonal, but on the last page he added the verses:

> To Mrs. Ann Flaxman
> A little Flower grew in a lonely Vale
> Its form was lovely but its colours pale
> One standing in the Porches of the Sun
> When his Meridian Glories were begun
> Leap'd from the steps of fire & on the grass
> Alighted where this little flower was
> With hands divine he mov'd the gentle Sod
> And took the Flower up in its native Clod
> Then planting it upon a Mountains brow
> 'Tis your own fault if you don't flourish now
> > William Blake.

On the evidence of these lines, and before the discovery of the letter referred to above, it had been conjectured that Blake gave the book to Mrs. Flaxman in return for her husband's part in introducing him to William Hayley and so effecting his removal in 1800 to Felpham in Sussex, where he could work gainfully under Hayley's patronage. This view dated the work to some year after 1800, even, it has been suggested, as late as 1805. The interpretation would identify the 'One standing in the Porches of the Sun' as Flaxman and the 'little flower' as Blake's artistic powers. Both images are unconvincing, and the further suggestion identifying the Felpham sea-side and Hayley's patronage as 'a Mountain's brow' is equally unsatisfying.

Moreover the guess overlooked the drawing which surrounds the panel carrying Blake's verses and which Blake entitled '12 A Spirit conducted to Paradise', a subject related only in a general way to the preceding poem, 'Elegy written in a Country Church-yard', and not to any particular line. The illustrations on every other page of the book are concerned, even if indirectly, with Gray's poems alone, but the last page, being blank, was perhaps used by Blake for a drawing with a double intention. The lightly drawn design shews a young man pointing upwards with one hand, while extending the other to draw after him the floating form of a woman with an eager expression on her face and her hands raised in expectancy. This could be taken to represent the spirit of Blake's creative powers introducing Ann Flaxman's delicate perceptions to a greater appreciation of poetry and design on the mountain of the double genius of Gray and Blake, the 'mountain' being a symbol often used by Blake to express spiritual elevation. It is possible that Blake composed and wrote the verses in this final blank panel as an afterthought, turning his simple drawing to another more personal purpose.

Flaxman's generous action was probably initiated by his sympathy for Blake in his disappointment at the failure of the designs for Young. It was part of his continual efforts to help his friend in a way that would not offend his self-esteem, though no record of the terms of the transaction has survived. Blake was a rapid worker and it is likely that the designs were completed in the early months of 1798. He is not known to have been engaged on any other major work at this time.

The subsequent history of the volume, in a contemporary half-calf binding, can soon be told. Mrs. Flaxman died in 1820 and her husband survived her by only six years. His effects were sold by Christie on 1 July 1828, the Gray volume (lot 85) being bought for eight guineas by 'Clarke', probably the dealer William Clarke of New Bond Street. The next owner was William Beckford of Fonthill Abbey, who already possessed a number of Blake's Illuminated Books. In 1810 Beckford's younger daughter Susan had married the Marquis of Douglas, afterwards tenth Duke of Hamilton, and it may be surmised that through this marriage Blake's illustrations to Gray came to rest with Beckford's library in the Duke's Scottish home at Hamilton Palace. Beckford's books were sold with many of the Hamilton collections in 1882, but the Blake volume was not included, possibly by an oversight. William Michael Rossetti had recorded its existence in 1863 in his list of Blake's works appended to Gilchrist's *Life of Blake*, but he described the designs as 'of unascertained method' and he certainly had not seen them. The whole series, indeed, remained virtually unknown until the book was rediscovered at the final dismantling of Hamilton Palace in 1919, when it was seen by H.J.C. (later Sir Herbert) Grierson, Regius Professor of Rhetoric and English Literature at Edinburgh University, who announced the discovery in a letter to *The Times* on 4 November. The Duke of Hamilton chose to keep this splendid volume in his private library, and by the kindness of the late Duchess, who much admired Blake's work, I was permitted to see it in her London home in December of that year. Publication had been suggested by Professor Grierson and opinions were taken as to whether the reproductions should be full size or reduced. I gave my vote for actual size and eventually the

Oxford University Press published in 1922 an elephant folio volume of reproductions in monochrome. Six of the pages were also done in colour-collotype facsimile as representative specimens and were inserted at the end. Professor Grierson, whose chief interests were literary, contributed a delightful and learned Introduction concerned with Gray's and Blake's poetry rather than with the illustrations, though making a number of penetrating observations on both. The original volume remained in the Duke of Hamilton's house at Lennoxlove and could be seen by visitors, though it was never included in any exhibition of Blake's works.

In February 1966 the volume passed into the possession of Mr. Paul Mellon and was transferred to the United States. Its new owner was anxious that this splendid example of Blake's work should be made available to a wider public and generously loaned the originals to Mr. Arnold Fawcus, of the Trianon Press in Paris, so that his firm could produce the hand-coloured facsimile to be published by them under the aegis of the William Blake Trust.

THE PLATES

On the following pages sixteen designs have been reproduced in colour and one in monochrome. Blake's handwritten title and corresponding manuscript number are given on the verso of each page. The design number is also given for easy reference to the Commentary.

At the end of the book, following the Commentary, the complete series of the designs is given in reduced monochrome.

ODE ON THE SPRING

Ms. no. 2   *Gray writing his Poems*
Design no. 2

2

Design   **Ode on the Spring**

1   The Pindaric Genius receiving his Lyre

2   Gray writing his Poems

3   The Purple Year awaking from the Roots of
     Nature, & the Hours suckling their
     Flowery Infants

4   "With me the Muse shall sit & think
     At ease reclind in rustic state"

5   "Brushd by the hand of rough Mischance
     Or chilld by Age"

6   Summer Flies reproaching the Poet

Around the Springs of Gray my wild root weaves
Traveller repose & Dream among my leaves

          Will. Blake

ODE

ON THE

SPRING.

LO! where the rosy-bosom'd hours,
  Fair VENUS' train, appear,
Disclose the long-expected flowers,
  And wake the purple year!
The Attic warbler pours her throat,
Responsive to the cuckow's note,
The untaught harmony of spring :
While, whisp'ring pleasure as they fly,
Cool Zephyrs thro' the clear blue sky
Their gather'd fragrance fling.

                    D   Where-

Ms. no. 3   *The Purple Year awaking from the Roots of Nature*
Design no. 3   *& The Hours suckling their Flowery Infants*

ODE

ON THE DEATH OF A

FAVOURITE CAT.

Drowned in a Tub of Gold Fishes.

D 3

Ms. no. 2   *'Demurest of the Tabby kind'*
Design no. 8

Ode on the Death of
a Favourite Cat

Design.

1. "Midst the tide
   Two Angel forms were seen to glide"

2. "Demurest of the Tabby kind"

3. "The pensive Selima
   Her ears of Jet & Emerald eyes
   She saw & purr'd applause"

4. "Still had she gaz'd but midst the tide
   Two Angel forms were seen to glide
   The hapless nymph with wonder saw
   A Whiskers first & then a Claw &c"

5. "Malignant Fate sat by & smil'd
   The slippery verge her feet beguil'd
   She tumbled headlong in"

6. "Nine times emerging from the flood
   She mew'd to every watry god"

O D E

ON THE DEATH OF A

FAVOURITE CAT.

Drowned in a Tub of Gold Fishes.

'TWAS on a lofty vase's side,
    Where China's gayest art had dy'd
  The azure flowers, that blow;
Demurest of the tabby kind,
  The pensive Selima reclin'd,
    Gaz'd on the lake below.

Her conscious tail her joy declar'd;
  The fair round face, the snowy beard,
    The velvet of her paws;
          D 4   Her

Ms. no. 3   '*The pensive Selima*
Design no. 9   *Her Ears of Jet & Emrald Eyes*
               She saw & purr'd applause'

Ms. no. 4   *'Still had she gazd but midst the tide*
Design no. 10   *Two Angel forms were seen to glide*
                        The hapless nymph with wonder saw
                        A Whisker first & then a Claw &c'

50   ODE ON THE DEATH

Her coat, that with the tortoife vies,
Her ears of jet, and emerald eyes,
   She faw; and purr'd applaufe.

Still had fhe gaz'd; but 'midft the tide
Two angel forms were feen to glide,
   The Genii of the ftream:
Their fcaly armour's Tyrian hue,
Thro' richeft purple to the view
   Betray'd a golden gleam.

The haplefs nymph with wonder faw:
A whifker firft, and then a claw,
   With many an ardent wifh,
She ftretch'd, in vain, to reach the prize.
What female heart can gold defpife?
   What cat's averfe to fifh?

                     Prefump-

OF A FAVOURITE CAT.   5₁

Presumptuous maid! with looks intent
Again she stretch'd, again she bent,
    Nor knew the gulph between:
(Malignant Fate sat by, and smil'd)
The slipp'ry verge her feet beguil'd,
She tumbled headlong in.

Eight times emerging from the flood
She mew'd to ev'ry wat'ry God,
    Some speedy aid to send.
No Dolphin came, no Nereid stirr'd.
Nor cruel Tom, nor Susan heard,
    A fav'rite has no friend!

From hence, ye beauties, undeceiv'd,
Know, one false step is ne'er retriev'd,
    And be with caution bold.

                        Not

Ms. no. 5   '*Malignant Fate sat by & smild*
Design no. 11   *The slippery verge her feet beguild*
               She tumbled headlong in'

Ms. no. 6   'Nine times emerging from the flood
Design no. 12   She mew'd to every watry God'

52   O D E,   &c.

Nor all that tempts your wand'ring eyes,
And heedlefs hearts, is lawful prize ;
   Nor all that glifters, gold.

O D E

Ms. no. 7   'Shaggy forms oer Ice built mountains roam'
Design no. 47

II. 2.

In climes beyond the folar road,
Where fhaggy forms o'er ice-built mountains
roam,
The Mufe has broke the twilight gloom,
To cheer the fhiv'ring native's dull abode.
And oft beneath the od'rous fhade
Of Chili's boundlefs forefts laid,
She deigns to hear the favage youth repeat
In loofe numbers wildly fweet
Their feather-cinctur'd chiefs, and dufky loves.
Her track, where-e'er the Goddefs roves,
Glory purfue, and gen'rous Shame,
Th' unconquerable mind, and Freedom's holy
flame.

II. 3.

Woods that wave o'er Delphi's fteep,
Ifles, that crown th' Egean deep,

Fields,

Save that from yonder ivy-mantled tower,
The moping owl does to the moon complain
Of such, as wand'ring near her secret bower,
Molest her ancient solitary reign.

Beneath those rugged elms, that yew-tree's shade,
Where heaves the turf in many a mouldring heap,
Each in his narrow cell for ever laid,
The rude Forefathers of the hamlet sleep.

The breezy call of incense breathing Morn,
The swallow twitt'ring from the straw-built shed,
The cock's shrill clarion, or the echoing horn,
No more shall rouse them from their lowly bed.

For them no more the blazing hearth shall burn,
Or busy housewife ply her evening-care;
No children run to lisp their sire's return,
Or climb his knees the envied kiss to share.

Oft

ELEGY WRITTEN IN A COUNTRY CHURCH-YARD

Ms. no. 4   *'For him no more the blazing hearth shall burn*
Design no. 108 *Nor children run to lisp their sires return'*

THE DESCENT OF ODIN

Ms. no. 10   *The Serpent & the Wolvish Dog—*
Design no. 86   *Two terrors in the Northern Mythology*

The Triumphs of Owen

1. A Standard bearer fainting in the routed battle

2. A Festal board

3. The Bard singing Owen's praise

4. "Dauntless on his native sands
The Dragon son of Mona stands"

5. "Fear to stop & shame to fly"

6. The Liberal Man inviting the traveller into his house

ODE ON A DISTANT PROSPECT OF ETON COLLEGE

Ms. no. 6   *Yet see how all around them wait*
Design no. 18   *The vultures of the Mind*

58 ODE ON A DISTANT PROSPECT

Theirs buxom Health, of rosy hue,
Wild wit, Invention ever-new,
And lively Cheer of Vigour born;
The thoughtless day, the easy night,
The spirits pure, the slumbers light,
That fly th' approach of morn.

Alas! regardless of their doom,
The little victims play!
No sense have they of ills to come,
Nor care beyond to-day:
Yet see, how all around 'em wait
The ministers of human fate,
And black Misfortune's baleful train!
Ah, show them where in ambush stand,
To seize their prey, the murderous band!
Ah, tell them they are men!

+ These shall the fury passions tear,
The vultures of the mind,
                              Disdainful

Difdainful Anger, palid Fear,
And Shame that fkulks behind;
Or pining Love fhall wafte their youth,
Or Jealoufy, with rankling tooth,
That inly gnaws the fecret heart:
And Envy wan, and faded Care,
Grim-vifag'd comfortlefs Defpair,
And Sorrow's piercing dart.

Ambition this fhall tempt to rife,
Then whirl the wretch from high,
To bitter fcorn a facrifice,
And grinning Infamy.
The ftings of Falfehood thofe fhall try,
And hard Unkindnefs alter'd eye,
That mocks the tear it forc'd to flow;
And keen Remorfe with blood defil'd,
And moody Madnefs laughing wild
Amid fevereft woe.

E   Lo,

Ms. no. 7   *Ambition this shall tempt to rise*
Design no. 19   *Then whirl the wretch from high &c*

A LONG STORY

Ms. no. 8   *'Out of the window whisk they flew'*
Design no. 30

So Rumour fays: (Who will, believe.)
But that they left the door a-jar,
Where, safe and laughing in his fleeve,
He heard the diftant din of war.

Short was his joy. He little knew
The power of magic was no fable;
Out of the window, whifk, they flew,
But left a fpell upon the table.

The words too eager to unriddle
The poet felt a ftrange diforder:
Tranfparent birdlime form'd the middle,
And chains invifible the border,

So cunning was the Apparatus,
The powerful pothooks did fo move him,
That, will he, nill he, to the Great-houfe
He went, as if the devil drove him.

　　　　　　　　　　　Yet

A LONG STORY.   71

Yet on his way (no sign of grace,
For folks in fear are apt to pray)
To Phœbus he preferr'd his case,
And begg'd his aid that dreadful day.

The Godhead would have back'd his quarrel,
But with a blush on recollection
Own'd that his quiver and his laurel
'Gainst four such eyes were no protection.

The Court was sat, the Culprit there,
Forth from their gloomy mansions creeping
The Lady *Janes* and *Joans* repair,
And from the gallery stand peeping:

Such as in silence of the night
Come (sweep) along some winding entry
(*Styack* has often seen the sight)
Or at the chapel-door stand sentry;

                                    In

Ms. no. 9   '*At the Chapel door stand centry*'
Design no. 31

THE PROGRESS OF POESY

Ms. no. 6   *'Hyperion's march they spy & glittering shafts of war'*
Design no. 46

85 THE PROGRESS OF POESY.

O'er her warm cheek, and rising bosom, move
The bloom of young desire, and purple light
    of Love.

II. 1.

Man's feeble race what ills await!
Labour, and Penury, the racks of Pain,
Disease, and Sorrow's weeping train,
And Death, sad refuge from the storms of Fate!
The fond complaint, my song, disprove,
And justify the laws of Jove.
Say, has he given in vain the heav'nly Muse?
Night, and all her sickly dews,
Her spectres wan, and birds of boding cry,
He gives to range the dreary sky:
Till down the eastern cliffs afar
Hyperion's march they spy, and glitt'ring
    shafts of war.

II. 2.

Oft did the harvest to their sickle yield,
Their furrow oft the stubborn glebe has broke:
How jocund did they drive their team afield!
How bow'd the woods beneath their sturdy stroke!

Let not Ambition mock their useful toil,
Their homely joys, and destiny obscure;
Nor grandeur hear with a disdainful smile,
The short and simple annals of the poor.

The boast of heraldry, the pomp of power,
And all that beauty, all that wealth e'er gave,
Await alike th' inevitable hour.
The paths of glory lead but to the grave.

Nor you, ye proud, impute to these the fault,
If Memory o'er their tomb no trophies raise,
Where thro' the long-drawn aisle and fretted vault,
The pealing anthem swells the note of praise.

Can

Commentary

Blake's manuscript titles are given in italics; the verses taken from Gray's lines are quoted exactly as Blake wrote them, including spelling and punctuation. The 116 designs have been allotted consecutive numbers; to assist identification the page number of Gray's text is also given. Blake numbered the illustrations of each poem separately, and these are referred to below as 'ms. no.'.

THE TITLE-PAGE

Design no. 1 (title-page, ms. no. [1])
The Pindaric Genius recieving his Lyre

William Blake introduces his illustrations to Gray's Poems with a design surrounding the title-page that depicts Genius mounted on a swan in full and splendid flight, exhibiting all the 'Energy' which was to Blake 'Eternal Delight', as he had reiterated in *The Marriage of Heaven and Hell* written a few years earlier.

ODE ON THE SPRING

Design no. 2 (verso of title-page, ms. no. 2)
Gray writing his Poems

The young poet is shewn seated with pen in hand and paper on knee, bathed in a beam of soft light emanating from an orb which must represent the Moon, symbol of Inspiration informed by Love, rather than from the Sun's creative furnace. His face is a recognizable image of Gray, and he is clothed in a pink robe, changed in later pictures to blue, though the colour does not seem to have any particular significance.

As already mentioned in the Introduction, Blake added to his list of titles for this poem the two lines:

> Around the Springs of Gray my wild root weaves
> Traveller repose & Dream among my leaves.
> —Will Blake

In these words Blake warns the observer that he is going to allow himself some licence in adding pictorial glosses of his own while illustrating Gray's poems. It will be seen that his 'wild roots' often draw curious nourishment from Gray's 'springs', and the results would sometimes have astonished the poet if he could have seen them. Blake invites the passer-by to stop and wonder what his pictures mean, with a pun on the word 'leaves'.

Design no. 3 (page 43, ms. no. 3)
The Purple Year awaking from the Roots of Nature
& The Hours suckling their Flowery Infants

The nude personification of 'the Purple Year' is balancing by hands and toes on 'the Roots of Nature', literally represented in the drawing. His bright curling hair is seen against the Sun's orb, whose genial warmth encourages the appearance of 'the long-expected flowers' of the previous line. This allusion allows Blake to indulge his fancy for humanization of natural objects, particularly flowers, in a most lovely and elaborate design.

Almost every line of Gray's first stanza is illustrated. Above, a huge Venus star, leader of the 'rosy-bosom'd hours', hangs from a tendril just below the point where a tiny 'Attic warbler pours her throat'. On the right, 'Cool Zephyrs thro' the clear blue sky / their gather'd fragrance fling'. Below and on the left, the 'rosy-bosom'd hours' release the flowering babes and suckle them in accordance with Blake's gloss in his description. The whole design is a riot of delicate beauty.

Design. no. 4 (page 44, ms. no. 4)
'With me the Muse shall sit & think
At ease reclind in rustic state'

The poet, now clad in a blue robe, is resting 'Beside some water's rushy brink', overshadowed by a dark rock and the trunk of a great tree with ivy climbing up it, Blake's usual symbol of the troubles of Experience. The Muse beside him has her eyes closed in thought.

Design no. 5 (page 45, ms. no. 5)
'Brush'd by the hand of rough Mischance
Or chilld by Age'

In this and the next illustration Blake has introduced many small personifications of Gray's phrase on the previous page, 'insect youth are on the wing', the poet having laid great stress on the flying harbingers of spring. Blake, in his own poem, 'Spring', in *Songs of Innocence*, had used birds, children and a lamb as his symbols. Now, he seems to illustrate also 'The Fly' in *Songs of Experience*. His title for the design may well have reminded him of his own first stanza:

Little fly
Thy summers play,
My thoughtless hand
Has brush'd away.

In his illustration to Gray the oafish figure of Mischance has crushed with heavy hands two tiny human flies, thus emphasizing Gray's idea by a stark picture of the human predicament. 'Contemplation' with his 'sober eye', a bearded figure in gown and hood, is standing apparently unmoved in the background, while flying figures, turned blue by cold, crouch on his shoulders or drop helplessly to the ground. Above, other human flies dance merrily in a ring. Another, rising on the left from the barren branches of the Tree of Life, blows a serpentine trumpet.

Design no. 6 (page 46, ms. no. 6)
Summer Flies reproaching the Poet

In this, as in the preceding illustration, Blake has characteristically added a fresh dimension to Gray's poem by his translation of the images into visual terms, thus driving home his warning. Gray, still in his blue robe, is reclining on the roots of a massive tree, forming a mirror image of 'the Purple Year awaking from the Roots of Nature' in the third illustration, but his state of mind is sharply contrasted. His face has a sullen expression, and Blake takes the opportunity to reproach him for his celibate life. Two pink-winged flies hover above him pointing derisive fingers. Others on the tree are nursing a baby or blowing a trumpet to illustrate the poet's own lines:

> Poor Moralist! and what art thou?
> A solitary fly!
> Thy joys no glitt'ring female meets,
>
>   . . .
>
> On hasty wings thy youth is flown;
> Thy sun is set, thy spring is gone—
> We frolic while 'tis May.

A warning of possible disaster is, however, attached to the drooping branches of the tree on the right in the form of a spider's web harbouring a menacing demon with a tiny sword.

ODE ON THE DEATH OF A FAVOURITE CAT
DROWNED IN A TUB OF GOLD FISHES

The illustrations to the second poem, 'On the Death of a Favourite Cat', are surely the most successful of the whole series. Blake was usually an accurate and literal illustrator, but could contribute highly significant touches of humour, irony and satire through his use of symbolism and personification, thus adding, in this instance, his own peculiar meaning to a seemingly trivial poem. Gray's Ode on the death of Horace Walpole's cat, Selima, by drowning in a tub of gold-fish was a *jeu d'esprit* with a suitably prim moral. Blake chose to illustrate it on more than one level, adding to the tragi-comedy a gloss containing a satire on woman with reflections on human error and regeneration.

> Design no. 7 (page 47, ms. no. 1)
>   '*Midst the tide*
>   *Two Angel forms were seen to glide*'

It is possible that Blake made the first two designs after he had completed the four for the body of the poem, the illustrations on the preliminary pages being of a general nature. Thus the design surrounding the fly-title to the poem depicts the feline aspect of feminine vanity and sexuality. Selima is shewn stretching out her claws over the water towards the 'angel forms'. Blake has ignored the details of the scene in Gray's lines. The 'lofty vase', or tub, containing the fish has become a limitless lake; the 'angel forms' are far from angelic, being transformed into fishy demons, able to arouse Selima's worst instincts of cruelty and greed by their resplendent red-gold colours. Their evil nature is betrayed by their hideous faces and

43

spiky bat-wings, their scaly armour suggesting the 'wat'ry Gods' of the sixth stanza. Selima herself is given not only human hands and feet with long claws, but is clothed in corset, shawl and turban. Her eye is red, not 'emerald' as in the poem. The sinister atmosphere of the whole is intensified by the superb drawing and colouring, adding a new meaning to Gray's slightly ironic verses.

Design no. 8 (page 48, ms. no. 2)
'Demurest of the Tabby kind'

On the verso of the fly-title Blake offers a complete contrast, picturing Selima as a demure 'tabby' stretched on the top of the panel containing his titles, in conformity with Gray's initial account of her. Her human counterpart appears as a little over-fed girl seated on her back. Two ordinary fish painted in sober colours swim below, each with an inoffensive and wingless 'angel form' riding on its back.

Design no. 9 (page 49, ms. no. 3)
'The pensive Selima
Her Ears of Jet & Emerald Eyes
She saw & purr'd applause'

For the title of the first illustration related directly to the poem Blake has taken lines from the first and second stanzas, but he has completely changed Gray's images into his own allegoric forms. Selima is frankly transformed into a pretty woman, though with a suspicion of whiskers on her face, pointed cat's ears and a tabby's tail flourished over the panel. Although female vanity is only covertly implied by Gray's description of her more attractive features in the second stanza, in Blake's illustration her conscious interest is concentrated on her own image reflected in the water and she is not noticing the fish. These have become a pair of naked human lovers, male and female with finny wings, embracing on the floor of the lake. They are hidden from Selima by the flowering water-plants suggested by Gray's opening lines:

> 'Twas on a lofty vase's side,
> Where China's gayest art had dy'd
> The azure flowers, that blow. . .

Design no. 10 (page 50, ms. no. 4)
'Still had she gazd but midst the tide
Two Angel forms were seen to glide
The hapless nymph with wonder saw
A Whisker first & then a Claw &c'

The fourth design is a partial repetition of the first introductory drawing, though in a much altered form. Selima above, and partly obscured by, the panel is now more cat than woman, though human feet are seen to protrude from beneath the cloak covering part of her body. Her attention has been diverted from her self-admiration to the 'angel forms' in the water, which are now the two lovers disporting themselves in joyous liberation after their experience of sexual union. Selima is excited by 'many an ardent wish', extending far beyond Gray's conventional observations:

> What female heart can gold despise?
> What cat's averse to fish?

Moreover the design anticipates a line on the following page, ' (Malignant Fate sat by, and smil'd)', Fate being represented by an old woman seated behind Selima ready with shears to cut the rope connecting her with earthly life.

Design no. 11 (page 51, ms. no. 5)

> '*Malignant Fate sat by & smild*
> *The slippery verge her feet beguild*
> *She tumbled headlong in*'

Blake has here diverged again from Gray's description of the ensuing tragedy. Selima has now become entirely human and she has been pushed head-first into the water by 'Malignant Fate'. The fish he has also transformed in two ways. He depicts them as warriors armed with spear and shield, the spears ironically furnished with fish-hooks attached to their points. The hunted are now exultant hunters, and at the same time they again represent the 'watr'y Gods' of Gray's sixth stanza, perhaps Neptune and his partner.

Design no. 12 (page 52, ms. no. 6)

> '*Nine times emerging from the flood*
> *She mew'd to every watry God*'

Blake has taken for this title to his final design two lines from Gray's sixth stanza on the preceding page but has significantly altered *eight* to *nine*, for the cat's nine lives of popular legend are finished, and she is now shewn as a woman in an attitude of prayer emerging from the water to enter a spiritual life in a new world. Below her a pair of perfectly indifferent gold-fish swim away unharmed. Gray's conventional moralizing has been transmuted into a barbed allegory of woman's frailty.

ODE ON A DISTANT PROSPECT OF ETON COLLEGE

In the third poem, 'On a Distant Prospect of Eton College', where Gray had spent the happiest days of his boyhood, Blake's ten designs depict both a boy's simple pleasures in the innocence of youth and the poet's warnings of what may follow in real life.

Design no. 13 (page 53, ms. no. 1)

Windsor terrace, a Boy contemplating a distant view of Eton College

In the first illustration a boy is leaning on the balustrade of the terrace at Windsor Castle contemplating the distant view of his college. The Thames, carrying a sailing boat, flows between the Castle and the College.

Design no. 14 (page 54, ms. no. 2)

A Boy flying a Kite

This innocent amusement was previously used by Blake in the second plate of 'The Ecchoing Green' in *Songs of Innocence*.

Design no. 15 (page 55, ms. no. 3)

Two Boys wandering in the woods by Eton College. The Shade of
Henry the Sixth is seen among the trees. 'Henrys holy shade.' line 4

The reference is to Henry the Sixth, Founder of the College; Blake has depicted 'Henrys shade'.

Design no. 16 (page 56, ms. no. 4)

'Say Father Thames for thou hast seen
Full many a sprightly race
Who foremost &c'

In the fourth design Blake painted the dignified presence of Father Thames leaning on an urn from which the river flows. He is watching over boys sporting on the river's bank or cleaving 'with pliant arms, thy glassy wave' under the shadow of Windsor Castle. The theme was taken from a pencil drawing done for a different purpose, though not otherwise developed.

Design no. 17 (page 57, ms. no. 5)

'The captive linnet'
The rolling circle'
murmuring labours' &c

The fifth design continues the survey of the pastimes of boyhood, shewing one boy bowling a hoop and another on the branch of a tree handing down a nest of fledgling birds to a girl below. This theme was previously used by Blake, with variations, in the second plate both of *The Marriage of Heaven and Hell* and of 'The Ecchoing Green' in *Songs of Innocence*. He never hesitated to repeat details from earlier compositions when it suited him to do so. In this instance its use was perhaps suggested by Gray's reference to 'The captive linnet' in the first line on the page. Another boy, intent on his book, relates to the fifth and sixth lines:

While some on earnest business bent
Their murm'ring labours ply.

Design no. 18 (page 58, ms. no. 6)

Yet see how all around them wait
The vultures of the Mind

After drawing this succession of mild scenes Blake startles the observer by his sixth illustration, one of the most bizarre and most striking of the series. In the foreground children are happily playing: there is a boy with a primitive cricket bat and another jumping and shouting with joy, a girl is catching a ball, while another dandles a doll in her arms, illustrating the lines:

Alas! regardless of their doom,
The little victims play!

though in his title Blake quotes two different non-consecutive lines. His spectres descend unseen onto the unsuspecting children, behind whom lurk the grisly company of 'black Misfortune's baleful train'. The elder Breughel had little advantage over Blake in the invention of grotesque forms of horror in semi-human shapes. One of the vultures, with long feminine arms and pendulous breast, reaches lustfully for a tender boy. The shapes behind them represent Jealousy, a bluish figure with a snake twined round his arm, Gluttony as a hog rooting in the ground, Anger as a leonine crouching beast, Avarice with some resemblance to Blake's famous image of 'The Ghost of a Flea', here folding a transparent arm round the second boy, Despair clasping her arms round the girl with a doll. On the right a green snake's head hangs over the children; a later illustration for the 'Ode for Music' (Design no. 95) shews that this symbolizes Flattery.

Design no. 19 (page 59, ms. no. 7)

Ambition this shall tempt to rise
Then whirl the wretch from high &c

The crowned figure of Ambition offers a palm frond to a youth climbing painfully up a steep crag to reach it, ignoring the bodies of two others fallen and falling from the top:

To bitter scorn a sacrifice,
And grinning Infamy.

Scorn and Infamy are pointing at the victims.

Design no. 20 (page 60, ms. no. 8)

Lo in the Vale of Years beneath
The painful family of Death

The monstrous figure of the Queen, entwined with serpents and grasping the emblems of punishment in her fists, is seated at the head of her train. Each foot is planted on a huge scarlet star-fish of uncertain significance. Above her are the shadowy grey figures of the relatives mourning for their dead. Brooding over the whole scene is a magnificent vision of a winged Urizen, Blake's personal symbol of the cruel creator of the material world, a striking example of a gloss by Blake adding effectively to the poet's intention.

Design no. 21 (page 61, ms. no. 9)

Where Ignorance is bliss
Tis folly to be wise

Blake pictures this familiar adage as a boy chasing a winged object with his cap, suggested by the line, 'And happiness too swiftly flies'.

He is unaware of the grinning image of Folly lodged in a tree above him. She is wafting the object of his pursuit ever further out of his reach with puffs of wind coming from phials in her hands.

Design no. 22 (page 62, ms. no. 10)

Boys playing at Top.

The Eton sequence ends with a peaceful scene. The branches of Blake's usual Tree of Life arch over the boys' heads. The panel is filled with Blake's manuscript list of titles for the illustrations of the next poem.

A LONG STORY

The fourth poem, with its mock-serious title, is a playful account of a visit paid to Gray's residence by two young women, Lady Schaub and Miss Speed. They had admired his 'Elegy written in a Country Church-yard' and had vowed to introduce the poet to their hostess, Lady Cobham, who was Gray's neighbour at the stately house of Stoke Poges Manor. Gray was out when they called (the poet pretended that the Muses had concealed him in 'a small closet in the garden'), so they wrote their names on a piece of paper and left it on the parlour table.

Gray soon came to know the family at the Manor and made a fanciful and amusing set of verses out of the incident. He imagined the two ladies as Amazons vowed to the duty of hunting out the poet, who is accused of bewitching the country children and putting spells on the farm animals and poultry. They accordingly burst into the house and, not finding him, ransacked the rooms. They finally flew out of a window, leaving a counter-spell on the table. The poet was summoned to a trial before a tribunal of 'high dames of honour' with the Peeress presiding. Having heard him confess that 'he once or twice had penn'd a sonnet', the Peeress, to the disgust of the tribunal, rose and gracefully bade him come to dinner.

Gray's harmlessly entertaining verses had been handed around in town, but were not approved of by some of his friends, and he therefore excluded them from his collected *Poems* published in 1768, but they were restored, with the authority of Gray's executor, William Mason, in the edition of 1790. Gray had introduced into his verses glimpses of fairyland and high life with touches of wit and fantasy. All of this was greatly appreciated by Blake, who entered into its spirit and made his twelve designs for the poem with obvious enjoyment.

Design no. 23 (page 63, ms. no. 1)

A Circular Dance

To launch the joke on the correct note Blake painted as his first design on the fly-title a kind of fairy ring of a nude youth and four damsels.

Design no. 24 (page 64, ms. no. 2)

Fairies riding on Flies

The verso of the fly-title carries the editor's explanation of the origin of the poem. Blake has surrounded this with drawings which carry on the theme of fairy-land. Below the panel is a large butterfly carrying a pink fairy; it has long curled antennae and yellow spots on its blue wings. On the left is a wasp with a tiny rider pointing a sting at the panel as if to suggest that the story does perhaps have rather more than a harmless joke hidden in it. Above, is a woman with four children, two of them playing musical instruments, perhaps representing free, impulsive creation, whereas the wasp indicates that Blake will enter more seriously than Gray into his satire on the attitude of high society to creative art.

Design no. 25 (page 65, ms. no. 3)
*'An ancient Pile of Building which
Employd the power of Fairy hands'*
In the third design, the first to illustrate the poem, Blake takes up Gray's fancy of the great house having been built by 'the power of Fairy hands', his exquisite little figures being shewn as employed on each craftsman's special task. The structure appears to be more like part of a Gothic cathedral than a dwelling house and the stained glass window, with its tracery and lightly sketched Christ figure, anticipates the design introducing the next poem but one, 'The Progress of Poesy'.

Design no. 26 (page 66, ms. no. 4)
' The Seals and Maces dancd before him'
The fourth design illustrates Gray's lines faithfully, though adding overtones of political feeling. A Tudor 'brawl', or dance, is in progress with Sir Christopher Hatton, Queen Elizabeth's Lord Keeper, in the lead. He is represented in an anachronistic costume of dandified elegance, with an Elizabethan ruff, a seventeenth century high-crowned hat set off by an enormous plume, and eighteenth century pants, finishing with high-heeled shoes tied with 'shoe-strings green'. He sniffs a rose and his ruff is conspicuously covered with spikes, indicative of a Satanic nature. The Great Seal and the Mace pirouette before him, both with indications of Blake's hatred of monarchical power. In 1798 he wrote in his annotations to Bacon's *Essays*, 'It was a Common Opinion in the Court of Queen Elizabeth that Knavery Is Wisdom'. The Mace is an evil-looking figure brandishing a massive staff with a bishop in its head. His partner, the Seal, is a frivolous little creature, crowned with a laurel wreath and having its ribbon continued into a devil's tail. The pillared arches in the background carry quartered shields in the spandrels.

Design no. 27 (page 67, ms. no. 5)
'A brace of warriors'
In the fifth illustration Blake introduces the 'warriors' as two charming young ladies elegantly dressed. Gray had described them as:
With bonnet blue and capuchin,
And aprons long they hid their armour. . .
In Blake's drawing one has a 'bonnet blue' with tall plumes, but the other wears a wide pink hat and waves a fan. Neither has a capuchin, which should resemble a monk's gown and hood.

Design no. 28 (page 68, ms. no. 6)
'Bewitchd the children of the Peasants'

49

The sixth design shews the wizard poet wearing a flowered gown and pink slippers while composing his spells to the terror of the village children and farm animals. The fence behind him is reminiscent of the Druid stones so often used by Blake elsewhere as symbols of the evils of religion.

Design no. 29 (page 69, ms. no. 7)

'Upstairs in a whirlwind rattle'

In the seventh design the warrior-ladies, having entered the house, terrorize the poet's mother and aunt beside their work table as they 'rattle' upstairs with ribbons flying.

Design no. 30 (page 70, ms. no. 8)

'Out of the window whisk they flew'

In the eighth, having ransacked the house in search of the poet, they fly out of the window leaving lightning flashes in their wake and 'a spell upon the table' in the guise of a letter summoning the poet to the 'Great-house'.

Design no. 31 (page 71, ms. no. 9)

'At the Chapel door stand centry'

The ninth design illustrates Gray's suggestion of ghosts roaming the Manor House:

Such as in silence of the night
Come (sweep) along some winding entry
(*Styack* has often seen the sight). . .

Blake portrays Styack, the housekeeper, terrified by a phantom with flaming eyes standing sentry at the chapel-door; it is portrayed so literally that it carries an immense rifle and bayonet against its shoulder.

Design no. 32 (page 72, ms. no. 10)

'A sudden fit of ague shook him'

In the tenth illustration the poet is seen, now properly dressed but shaken with 'a sudden fit', standing speechless before the tribunal of ancient ladies, whose facial types and head-dresses are carefully conceived, as in the well-known picture of 'The Canterbury Pilgrims', to be true for all time. Here they ridicule 'all the People of condition'. The Peeress, Lady Cobham, wearing an extravagant hat, sits above in judgement.

Design no. 33 (page 73, ms. no. 11)

*'My Lady rose & with a grace
She smild & bid him come to dinner'*

In the eleventh design, the poet having confessed that 'He once or twice had penn'd a sonnet', the Peeress steps down from her seat with a smile to invite the surprised culprit to dinner. The three dames, whose carefully drawn faces express their horror at the result of the trial, are those at the end of the row covered on the previous page by the panel for the text.

50

Design no. 34 (page 74, ms. no. 12)
'Guard us from long winded lubbers
That to Eternity would sing
And keep My Lady from her rubbers'
In the twelfth and last design the laurel-crowned poet reciting his Odes is received with alarm or boredom by 'the quality' sitting at their card table. Throughout this sequence Blake has entered whole-heartedly into the joke, but ends with a satirical picture of how polite society receives the serious artist.

ODE TO ADVERSITY

In the six illustrations to 'Ode to Adversity' Blake has toned down the colour of all of them to create a general impression of sadness. His liberal use of grey and blue washes leads up to the gloomy horrors of Adversity's Gorgon head and to her 'form benign'.

Design no. 35 (page 75, ms. no. 1)
A Widower & children
The introductory design is drab and rather uninteresting. Resignation in misfortune is expressed by all the figures beside the tombstone.

Design no. 36 (page 76, ms. no. 2)
Grief among the roots of trees
Not having any particular line of poetry to illustrate Blake has allowed his mind to revert to images used in his Illuminated Books a few years earlier. Grief is seen as a woman encysted, as it were, in a cavity formed of the roots of a massive tree. She is offering her breast to an infant which is dead. The tree and its neighbours have already been felled and an axe is about to sever even the root forming the refuge where she is hidden. A tree had many symbolic connotations in Blake's mind, from the Tree of the Knowledge of Good and Evil to the Tree of Mystery or of Crucifixion and Death. Here the image suggests the power for evil of the material world from which no refuge is safe, so connecting it with the general theme of adversity.

Design no. 37 (page 77, ms. no. 3)
'Purple tyrant vainly groans'
The design for the first page of the poem illustrates the greater part of the first stanza. Blake's image of the 'purple tyrant' bound in Adversity's 'adamantine chain' is related to his design on the thirteenth plate in his book, *Europe, A Prophecy*, 1794, shewing a youth in prison suffering the actuality of Experience.

Design no. 38 (page 78, ms. no. 4)
'Stern rugged Nurse'
Virtue Nursd in the Lap of Adversity
The grim figure of Adversity holds in her right hand Newton's compass, Blake's symbol of

51

the limitations of the material world, and in her left the Book of the Law, embodying life's negations. Her face, though stern, expresses an infinite pity for the sufferings of her nursling. Virtue, with tear-drops on her cheek, has a pen in her hand and a book on her knee, but it is not open and she appears to be writing on the cover. She is young and tender and is recording the title of the Book of Experience.

Design no. 39 (page 79, ms. no. 5)

'In thy Gorgon terrors clad
Screaming horror's funeral cry
Despair & Fell Disease & Ghastly Poverty'

The fifth design is the culmination of Gray's appeal for mercy. Blake pictures the 'Gorgon terrors' of Adversity and her 'vengeful band'. Suicidal Despair brandishing two daggers is on the left. In the foreground Fell Disease is emptying her pitcher of foul yellow waters; on the right, hollow-eyed Poverty threatens his victims with a scourge in either hand.

Design no. 40 (page 80, ms. no. 6)

'Oh gently on thy suppliant's head
Dread Goddess lay thy chastening hand'

Blake's title is taken from the previous page. He now pictures Adversity in her 'form benign', as addressed by the poet on the present page. She is habited like a nun in grey, and is administering philosophic consolation to a man immersed in thoughts of his own sorrow.

THE PROGRESS OF POESY. A PINDARIC ODE

The verso for the fly-title of this poem (covered by Blake with a slip of paper on which he wrote his titles for the illustrations) contains an Advertisement that states:

> When the author first published this and the following ode, he was advised, even by his friends, to subjoin some few explanatory notes; but he had too much respect for the understanding of his readers to take that liberty.

Nevertheless, Gray overcame his reluctance and in the 1768 collected edition and in the subsequent edition which Blake used, there are some useful notes for this poem as well as for certain others.

Design no. 41 (page 81, ms. no. 1)

The Beginning of Poesy. The blind begging Bard

Blake had probably noticed Gray's mention in the notes of Pindar's description of his poetry as, 'Aeolian song, Aeolian strings, the breath of the Aeolian flute', and in his preliminary drawing has emphasized the relation of Gray's Ode to Greek poetry by depicting an image of Homer, 'the blind begging Bard', led by a boy whose face expresses the utmost respect.

Design no. 42 (page 82, ms. no. 2)

Study

The second illustration is not related to any line by Gray, but shews the poet in a blue robe seated with an open book on his knee. He is in a chamber resembling that provided for the building of the Manor House at the beginning of 'A Long Story'. It has pillared arches and a large Gothic stained glass window containing a design of a many-winged cherub, below which is a seated Muse with pen and scroll gazing upwards for inspiration. The poet is conspicuously different from the inspired figure of 'Gray writing his Poems' drawn at the beginning of the volume. There he was illuminated by a beam of moonlight; now he is an older man reading what has been written by others in preparation for his study of 'The Progress of Poesy', a subject dear to the hearts of both poet and artist. The views of Gray, the Augustan, may be compared with Blake's much freer, less conventional, treatment of the succeeding poems of the prophetic 'Bard' and the other Welsh and Scandinavian themes.

Design no. 43 (page 83, ms. no. 3)

'The Laughing flowers that round them blow
Drink life & fragrance as they flow

The illustration to the first lines of Gray's text shews the waters of 'Helicon's harmonious springs' and 'The laughing flowers' drinking 'life and fragrance' from the stream. The 'rich stream of music' is personified by the figure of a Grecian woman with her lyre. She typifies the 'quiet majestic progress' of poetry described by Gray in his notes as flowing from the various sources of poetry.

Design no. 44 (page 84, ms. no. 4)

'Perching on the Scepterd hand
Of Jove, thy magic lulls the featherd king'

The fourth design illustrates Gray's lines describing the Eagle of War, subdued, as the poet explains in his notes, by the 'Power of harmony to calm the turbulent passions of the soul', the thought being borrowed from Pindar. The great bird is perched on Jove's forearm. Jove is a huge oppressive figure, whose right hand is resting on a sceptre, its massiveness emphasized by the acorns and oak leaves decorating its head. His left elbow rests on a large truncated column. The weight of the whole conception is relieved only by the line of dancing figures embroidered on the hem of Jove's robe.

Design no. 45 (page 85, ms. no. 5)

'Cytherea's Day'

The fifth design provides a happy contrast with the image of Jove on the previous page by its nine dancing figures, advancing on the left and retiring on the right, while waving tambourines over their heads. A winged boy with a violin and two maidens playing flutes are in attendance. Graceful trees arch over their heads and a huge Venus star hangs in the centre.

Blake is illustrating not only the lines of the poem, but also Gray's note on the 'Power of harmony to produce all the graces of motion in the body'. His lines,

>To brisk notes in cadence beating,
>Glance their many-twinkling feet.

are referred by Gray to a passage from Homer's *Odyssey*.

Design no. 46 (page 86, ms. no. 6)
'Hyperion's march they spy & glittering shafts of war'
The dance greeting the approach of Queen Cytherea in the soft twilight before the dawn leads on to the magnificent vision of 'Hyperion's march' in this design.

Blake's brilliant conception of Hyperion, the Bowman, fills the eye with a blaze of colour. He is seated in a sort of aerial chariot fringed with the shafts of war, which at the same time are rays of sunlight dispelling below the chariot 'Night's spectres wan', their grey protesting heads setting off the burst of light above. Blake's conception of the Sun, symbol of imagination and poetry, dispelling the gloom and terrors of night would also suggest victory over the evils of materialism.

The first conception of the Hyperion design is seen in a pencil drawing of 'The Bowman', with the spirit of Inspiration hovering overhead, reproduced in the Blake Trust facsimile. No preliminary drawings done expressly for the Gray illustrations are known for certain. 'The Bowman' and 'Father Thames', already mentioned, seem to have been drawn for other purposes. It is likely that Blake's rapid flow of ideas allowed him to dispense with careful studies; the style of many of the water-colour drawings suggests a quick action of pencil and brush, as if too much thought might spoil the immediacy of his imagination.

Design no. 47 (page 87, ms. no. 7)
'Shaggy forms oer Ice built mountains roam'
In the seventh design Blake has followed Gray's line closely. He may have been attracted by the idea that the liberty of primitive people was productive of true poetic inspiration, and his 'savage youth', clad in a shaggy wolf's skin, looks like a worthy product of 'Th' unconquerable mind, and Freedom's holy flame.'

Design no. 48 (page 88, ms. no. 8)
'Alike they scorn the pomp of Tyrant power
And coward Vice that revels in her chains
Gray describes in this section of the Ode the progress of poetry from Greece to Italy and from Italy to England in pursuit of liberty. The eighth illustration depicts the Nine Muses leaving 'their Parnassus for the Latian plains'. They float away from the dignified, though commonplace, figure of Tyranny with crown and sceptre, who is instructing the witless activities of Vice with his laurel wreath and ass's ears as he brays some discordant song, with one hand playing on a harmonium and a finger of the other stuck in his ear to keep out the sound. This is probably a covert satire on the reigning Poet Laureate, chained to state policy. The

whole design appears to express Blake's view of the effect of political tyranny on the state of poetry in England.

Design no. 49 (page 89, ms. no. 9)

'To him the mighty Mother did unveil
Her awful Face'

The ninth design illustrates Gray's section describing the rise of Shakespearian poetry. Mother Nature leans out of an enormous golden bowl over 'the dauntless child', kneeling naked beside the Avon. In her hand are the golden keys which will unlock the 'gates of Joy'. In the foreground Sympathy is emptying her bowl of tears into the stream of 'lucid Avon'.

Design no. 50 (page 90, ms. no. 10)

'Dryden.
'Bright Eyd Fancy hovering o'er'

The tenth illustration is devoted to Dryden, who is sitting on an elaborately wrought stool with a decorated lyre in his hands while 'Bright-eyed Fancy':

Scatters from her pictur'd urn
Thoughts that breathe, and words that burn.

Tongues of flame are issuing from the mouth of the urn, carrying with them 'breathing thoughts', pictured as young women with various gifts in their hands. The first one has released a singing bird into the air, the next one offers a grasshopper (representing, for Blake, vermin, one of the plagues of Egypt); a third has a snake in either hand, one of them apparently just emerging from an egg, while a fourth bears a sprig of laurel. The theme of Dryden's laureateship is further emphasized by a wreath round the neck of the urn and a little picture on its body of a tiny figure being crowned with laurel. All these thoughts symbolize the various strains of poetry composed by Dryden, such as his satires and the wasted areas of his attempts to 'revise' the works of greater poets (Chaucer, Milton, Shakespeare). Behind Fancy is part of a rainbow which carries over into the next design.

Design no. 51 (page 91, ms. no. 11)

Oft before his Infant eyes would run
Such forms as glitter in the Muses ray

Here the poet, in this case probably Gray himself, is shewn as a youth standing beneath the rainbow within which are seen, 'Such forms as glitter in the Muse's ray'.

The sky below is stormy and is pouring rain onto a field of flattened wheat on which the body of a youth is lying face down. This is difficult to interpret, but is reminiscent of a subject used on plate 9 of *America* (1794), shewing the new-born man lying asleep among luxuriant ears of corn, that is, the riches of this world. Blake was, perhaps, casting his mind back to Gray's earlier line, referring to Shakespeare, 'In thy green lap has Nature's darling laid', or perhaps it is a reference of sympathy for the death of Gray's friend, Richard West, in 1742.

55

Design no. 52 (page 92, ms. no. [12])

A Muse

Blake has decorated the next leaf with a generalized vision of a Muse with her lyre. The manuscript number has been omitted from the design, perhaps not unintentionally as the Muse appears to be in flight towards the subject of the next poem, 'The Bard'. The panel has been used for the titles of this poem.

THE BARD. A PINDARIC ODE

It has been suggested in the Introduction that 'The Bard' may have been the key poem that first opened Blake's mind to the splendour of Gray's poetry. It is certain that Blake was now intensely interested in the aspect of Gray's Bard-figure as the mythical poet-prophet of ancient times as well as being the prototype of his own position in the poetic world. He had announced his claim in the 'Introduction' to *Songs of Experience*, 1794:

> Hear the voice of the Bard!
> Who Present, Past, & Future sees
> Whose ears have heard,
> The Holy Word,
> That walk'd among the ancient trees.

It was the function of the poet-prophet to know the future and to tell the truth about past and present; also to divine the unconscious emotions of other men and to be the intermediary between the material world and the visionary world of the imagination. Blake saw in Gray's splendid Ode many opportunities for clothing these ideas with visible shapes and so producing a more intimate marriage between Gray's mind and his own than is to be found anywhere else in this book. To achieve his purpose in making an ordered series of painted images he had to do some violence to the sequence of the pages, illustrating the title-page of the poem (Design no. 53, ms. no. 1) from lines taken from page 96, the Advertisement page (Design no. 54, ms. no. 2) from lines taken from page 98, and the first illustration of the poem itself (Design no. 55, ms. no. 3) from later lines on page 98.

The Bard's message was one of revenge and revolution, and it is likely that the symbolism in some of the designs with historical implications can be related to Blake's feelings about the political situation in England at the time when he was working on this series.

Design no. 53 (page 93, ms. no. 1)

A Welch Bard

The design repeats to some extent the image of the Bard in the illustration to 'The Voice of the Ancient Bard' in *Songs of Experience*. There the ancient man is plucking the strings of his prophetic harp surrounded by young people eager to hear 'the Image of truth new born'. In the present design which illustrates the lines,

> On a rock, whose haughty brow
> Frowns o'er old Conway's foaming flood,
> Robed in the sable garb of woe,
> With haggard eyes the Poet stood. . .

the Bard is standing alone with his silent instrument at the edge of the 'Sea of Time and Space'. His special powers are announced by his starry magician's robe and by the angelic figure fashioned at the tip of his great golden harp, herself playing on a smaller instrument as an assurance that the message comes from God.

Design no. 54 (page 94, ms. no. 2)
The Slaughterd Bards, taken from the line
'The famishd Eagle screams & passes by' Page 98

In addition to the line quoted by Blake, the painting also illustrates Gray's Advertisement on its own page:

> The following Ode is founded on a Tradition current in Wales, that Edward the First, when he completed the conquest of that country, ordered all the Bards that fell into his hands to be put to death.

Thus the eagle, starved through the ravaging of the land by war, screams at the sight of the broken harp, symbolic of the frustration of poetic inspiration, and at the dead bodies of the three other Bards representing the Present, Past and Future of Blake's 'Introduction' to *Songs of Experience*. The Present, a young man with bright hair, lies with his face buried in the grass of the present vegetable world; the Past is a gigantic figure with a streaming white beard lying on his back and the Future is also on his back. The fate of these poets is an image of what might happen to an outspoken critic such as Blake in the England of 1797.

Design no. 55 (page 95, ms. no. 3)
The Bard weaving Edwards fate

The third design achieves, perhaps, the highest level of illustrative art to be seen in this book. The line illustrated, 'And weave with bloody hands the tissue of thy line', was taken from page 98 of the book where it is marked with two crosses. Blake has made his intention clear by repeating the crosses on the upper left corner of the present design.

The warp of Edward's fate is here pictured as part of a gigantic lyre, the strings being thickened to the size and appearance of huge shaggy ropes dripping with blood. The Bard's expression is sorrowful, but he plucks the strings as if to make the terrible tones of his message foretell Edward's downfall. There are no small details to distract attention from the terror of his prophecy.

Design no. 56 (page 96, ms. no. 4)
Edward & his Queen & Nobles astonishd at the Bards Song

This design pictures King Edward and his Queen, with their warriors, gazing upwards in alarm at the Bard's voice threatening them from the mountain above.

Design no. 57 (page 97, ms. no. 5)
'Hark how each Giant Oak & Desart Cave
Sigh to the Torrents awful voice beneath'

The personifications of oak trees, cave and torrent are effected with skill to make a composition of great power and balance.

Design no. 58 (page 98, ms. no. 6)
'On yonder Cliff. 'I see them sit'

In the sixth design the avenging bards are depicted as described in Gray's lines:
'On yonder cliffs, a griesly band,
I see them sit, they linger yet,
Avengers of their native land:
With me in dreadful harmony they join. . .'

Design no. 59 (page 99, ms. no. 7)
'O'er thy country hangs' The scourge of heaven'

The avenger of the murdered Edward II is his son, Edward III. He wields a scourge with three thongs armed with iron spikes over the cowering victims,
'Amazement in his van, with flight combin'd,
And Sorrow's faded form, and Solitude behind. . .'
the terrors in Gray's poem that 'round him wait'. The reference, as Gray points out in his notes, is to the disappointments and loneliness of the end of Edward III's reign. Amazement, flight and Sorrow are clearly depicted. Solitude is a tiny figure faintly pencilled far in the rear on the left of the landscape.

Design no. 60 (page 100, ms. no. 8)
The Whirlwind. 'Hushd in grim repose'

This strange personification of the Whirlwind follows accurately the lines of the poem:
'In gallant trim the gilded vessel goes;
Youth on the prow, and pleasure at the helm;
Regardless of the sweeping Whirlwind's sway,
That, hush'd in grim repose, expects his evening-prey.'
A ship is riding in calm waters by the light of the rising sun. The Whirlwind lies asleep on his windy bed, his curled horn on his arm ready to raise the hurricane when he awakes; protruding from his lips are the remains of the last victim he has devoured. The reference, as Gray points out again in his notes, is to the brilliant commencement of Richard II's reign and his violent end at the hands of Henry of Lancaster.

Design no. 61 (page 101, ms. no. 9)

'Fell thirst & Famine scowl
A baleful smile upon their baffled guest'

The ninth design covers a long period of English history. At the top are seen the embattled warriors of the Wars of the Roses, 'Lance to lance, and horse to horse'. On the right there is a boar, the device of Richard III, which wallows 'in infant gore'. The greater part of the painting is occupied by the figure of Richard II in Pontefract Castle starving to death in his 'regal chair'. Thirst holds an empty goblet turned upside down. Famine points to stones simulating bread on the ground before the King.

Design no. 62 (page 102, ms. no. 10)

The Death of Edwards Queen Eleanor from this line
'Half of thy heart we consecrate'

The King bends sorrowfully over his dying Queen. Their horses are behind him. Simulacra of the three Bards brood over them from the clouds above.

Design no. 63 (page 103, ms. no. 11)

Elizabeth. 'Girt with many a Baron bold'

A fair-featured Queen Elizabeth appears at the top of this design, crowned with oak leaves. Gray's Barons, wearing plumed helmets, are on the Queen's right. Her ruff is conspicuously spiked, shewing again Blake's hatred of the Monarchy. The three figures below are once more Present, Past and Future, their presence confirming the identification of their counterparts in the second illustration of this sequence. Present is looking towards the Queen, Past and Future look towards the reader, the latter holding a lyre with his fingers on the strings ready to prophesy.

Design no. 64 (page 104, ms. no. 12)

Spenser creating his Fairies.

On the text page surrounded by this design Blake has marked with a cross the line, 'And Truth severe, by fairy Fiction drest', words which could be applied to a number of his illustrations. Here Blake has taken Spenser as the type of creative poet, with his *Fairy Queen* as the outcome. The poet is seated in the centre with a fairy figure standing on his hand. He is watching intently three other figures on the ground acting out a scene from his poem, 'Sir Guyon in the cave of Mammon'. Above them is another group in a scene illustrating the episode of 'Redcrosse in the cave of Despair'. On the right of the picture are the forms of Truth, a young woman with an open book, and Fiction holding a scroll. Fiction's collar is spiked, a common convention with Blake when drawing fairy characters, since they have some relation to the powers of darkness. Over their heads are two figures making music with flute and pipe.

Design no. 65 (page 105, ms. no. 13)

'Headlong from the Mountains height
Deep in the roaring tide he plungd to endless night'

The Bard's grim prophecy of revenge is ended. His robe is no longer decorated with stars. His white diaphanous form plunges, with lyre in hands, into a black sea at the foot of a rugged cliff.

Design no. 66 (page 106, ms. no. [14])

A poor Goatherd in Wales.

The design on the verso of the last page of the 'Bard' is not related to any particular line of the poem. The goatherd is seated with a melancholy expression under the arching branch of a tree and is laying down his pipe. The tree, as often in Blake's mind, symbolizes the miseries of material existence. His goats graze unconcernedly by his side. The mountains of Wales, the setting of the previous poem, raise their dark shapes in the background. Blake has used the panel to list his titles for the next poem.

THE FATAL SISTERS. AN ODE

The sub-title to this Ode states that it is 'From the Norse Tongue' and is to be found in various authorities. In his Advertisement Gray calls this poem and the two that follow 'imitations', and in his Preface relates the legend on which the Ode is based:

In the eleventh century, *Sigurd*, Earl of the Orkney islands, went with a fleet of ships, and a considerable body of troops, into Ireland, to the assistance of *Sigtryg with the silken beard*, who was then making war on his father-in-law *Brian*, King of Dublin. The Earl and all his forces were cut to pieces, and *Sigtryg* was in danger of a total defeat; but the enemy had a greater loss, by the death of *Brian*, their King, who fell in the action. On Christmas-day, (the day of the battle,) a native of *Caithness* in Scotland saw, at a distance, a number of persons on horseback, riding full speed towards a hill, and seeming to enter into it. Curiosity led him to follow them; till looking through an opening in the rocks, he saw twelve gigantic figures resembling women: they were all employed about a loom, and as they wove, they sung the following dreadful song; which when they had finished, they tore the web into twelve pieces, and, each taking her portion, galloped six to the north, and as many to the south.

Design no. 67 (page 107, ms. no. 1)

The Three Fatal Sisters

The painting shews three gigantic women, each wearing a golden cuirass; those at left and right carry a huge spear. By shewing only three of the Sisters Blake is identifying them with the three Fates.

Design no. 68 (page 108, ms. no. 2)

A Muse

Blake has decorated the Advertisement page with a massive winged figure.

Design no. 69 (page 109, ms. no. 3)

Sigtryg with the Silken beard

The first page of the Preface is occupied with a painting of Sigtryg. He is clad in armour and holds a huge shield and spear.

Design no. 70 (page 110, ms. no. 4)

'Persons of [sic] Horseback riding full speed toward
a hill & seeming to Enter into it'

The second page of the Preface shews 'the native of Caithness' startled by the sight of 'persons on horseback riding full speed'. The riders are wearing red dresses and are presumably women.

Design no. 71 (page 111, ms. no. 5)

'Iron sleet of arrowy shower
Hurtles in the darkend air'

The Three Sisters, now in blue dresses, are weaving at a 'loom', but their threads are great arrow-pointed shafts, recalling the lines of the poem which follow those quoted in Blake's caption:

Glitt'ring lances are the loom,
Where the dusky warp we strain. . .

Design no. 72 (page 112, ms. no. 6)

'Shafts for shuttle dipd in gore
Shoot the trembling cords along'

Blake's design adds gruesome details taken from earlier on the page:

See the grisly texture grow!
('Tis of human entrails made,)
And the weights that play below,
Each a gasping warrior's head.

Design no. 73 (page 113, ms. no. 7)

'We the reins to slaughter give'

Blake illustrates this line with a battle-piece of horsemen galloping over the slain.

Design no. 74 (page 114, ms. no. 8)

The Fatal Sisters riding thro the Battle. they are calld
in some Northern poems 'Choosers of the Slain'

The Sisters are shown riding majestically over agonized bodies, pointing with out-stretched hands to the victims they have chosen. The victim on the left, wearing the remnants of a crown, evidently refers to the line which Blake has marked with a cross, 'soon a king shall bite the ground'. The design may also be taken to illustrate the lines:

> Sisters, weave the web of death.
> Sisters, cease: The work is done.

The subject is explained by Gray in a note:

> The *Valkyriur* were female divinities, servants of *Odin* (or *Woden*) in the Gothic mythology. Their name signifies *Chusers of the slain*. They were mounted on swift horses, with drawn swords in their hands; and in the throng of battle selected such as were destined to slaughter, and conducted them to *Valhalla*, (the hall of *Odin*, or paradise of the brave,) where they attended the banquet, and served the departed heroes with horns of mead and ale.

Design no. 75 (page 115, ms. no. 9)

'Hurry Hurry to the field'

The Sisters are pictured as about to mount their horses to set out for the battle.

Design no. 76 (page 116, ms. no. 10)

A Battle

Throughout this series it is plain that Blake, a hater of war and violence (though often employing images of violence in his own Prophetic Books), was chiefly interested in insuring that his illustrations should be impressive pictures of Gray's embattled lines. They contain nothing of his characteristic touches, symbolic or fanciful. In the last design of the poem, Blake has made a finely imagined pattern of war and slaughter, as if to emphasize his dislike of the whole theme. This surrounds one of the two panels which have been left blank.

THE DESCENT OF ODIN. AN ODE

Design no. 77 (page 117, ms. no. 1)

The Serpent who girds the Earth

Blake has illustrated the title-page of this Ode with a fine example of one of his favourite symbols, a Serpent, with horrific effect. It was for him the symbol of evil in many shapes, all stemming from the seductive corruptor of Eve in Paradise. In *The Four Zoas* it is the Prester Serpent calling forth the warriors to war (Night Seventh, lines 114-120). In some poems a serpent represents the priesthood, since Blake disliked organized religion; elsewhere the Serpent Temples, adopted from the eighteenth century antiquaries, stand for the cruel religion of the Druids. Sometimes the Serpent means the worship of Nature, or even Nature herself, at others it has the more traditional meaning of Eternity. In the present context this symbol seems to suggest both War and Nature, and is a suitable introduction to the sultry lines of Gray's poem in imitation of the Norse legend.

Design no. 78 (page 118, ms. no. 2)

Spectres

The space surrounding Blake's list of titles is occupied by three 'Spectres', unpleasant reminders of Nature in the shapes of winged apparitions reminiscent of similar 'butterflies' seen in the last illustration to 'Ode on the Spring' and the second to 'A Long Story'. The insect at the top is a summary sketch; that on the left, with a fairy riding on its back, is given added point by having its wings studded with stars, the machinery of the universe, and large ocellations. The third, below, gives a feeling of real horror with its dusky animal face, menacing claws and vampire wings. Its flight is urged on by the smirking nude woman on its back.

Design no. 79 (page 119, ms. no. 3)

'Him the Dog of Darkness spied'

Odin, the King of Men, riding towards the Gates of Hell, meets the dog of darkness, presumably corresponding to Cerberus of classical mythology. Odin is mounted on his 'coal-black steed' and brandishes a sword. The horse's head is almost a replica of the head in the picture of 'Nightmare' by Blake's friend, Fuseli, painted in 1783. In fact the whole sequence for this poem has the look of a pastiche of Fuseli's style in the exaggeration of limbs and attitudes.

Design no. 80 (page 120, ms. no. [4])

'Right against the eastern gate
By the mossgrown Pile he sat.'

In this design Odin has reached the mouth of Hell. He is tracing with the point of his sword 'a Runic rhyme' over the grave of 'the prophetic Maid'. Flames arise round it from the ground.

Design no. 81 (page 121, ms. no. 5)

The Prophetess Rising from her Grave

Blake's title sufficiently describes this very powerful design.

Design no. 82 (page 122, ms. no. 6)

'Tis the Drink of Balder bold'

The Prophetess, asked by Odin 'For whom yon glitt'ring board is spread', answers in the scene pictured by Blake:

> Mantling in the goblet see
> The pure bev'rage of the bee;
> O'er it hangs the shield of gold:
> 'Tis the drink of *Balder* bold.

Design no. 83 (page 123, ms. no. 7)

'A wondrous boy shall Rinda bear
Who neer shall comb his raven hair

Nor wash his visage in the stream
Till he on Hoders corse shall smile'

In Blake's design the 'wondrous boy', his mission completed, is seen combing his 'raven hair' seated on a rock at the edge of a lake, with a setting sun in the background.

Design no. 84 (page 124, ms. no. 8)
'Ha! No traveller art thou
King of Men I know thee Now'

The Prophetess and Odin stand facing one another, as the latter's identity is revealed.

Design no. 85 (page 125, ms. no. 9)
'Hie thee hence'

Odin mounts his horse and is dismissed by the Prophetess while she sinks again into the ground. Tongues of flame arise on either side.

Design no. 86 (page 126, ms. no. 10)
The Serpent & the Wolvish Dog—two terrors in the Northern Mythology

Surrounding the list of subjects for the next poem is one of the most terrifying designs in the book. Blake's Serpent and Wolvish Dog actually repeat in a different form two of the terrors seen in the first two illustrations for this poem.

Blake produced in this sequence a set of illustrations which may be compared with those made for Dante's *Divine Comedy* at the end of his life. They may seem crude in comparison with the beauty and subtlety of the later series, but they are more suited to the primitive Norse mythology than Blake's later style would have been.

THE TRIUMPHS OF OWEN. A FRAGMENT

Design no. 87 (page 127, ms. no. 1)
A Standard bearer fainting in the routed battle

This fragmentary 'imitation' of 'Mr. Evans's Specimen of Welsh Poetry' afforded Blake little opportunity for inventing themes of interest. The first design of a standard bearer does not illustrate any particular line in the poem and seems to suggest that Blake was tiring of the many scenes of violence.

Design no. 88 (page 128, ms. no. 2)
A Festal board

This design may be intended to illustrate the last two lines on the next page:
Lord of every regal art,
Liberal hand, and open heart.
All the lines of this page are in praise of Owen.

Design no. 89 (page 129, ms. no. 3)
The Bard singing Owens praise

Blake is again able to portray his Bard, clothed as before in his blue star-spangled robe, but now seated beside his Harp.

Design no. 90 (page 130, ms. no. 4)

'Dauntless on his native sands
The Dragon son of Mona stands'

Blake has drawn another fine battle-piece, painting it with good effect entirely in black and grey washes except for the warrior's 'ruby crest', that is, the plumes on his helmet, and a pink tinting on two faces.

Design no. 91 (page 131, ms. no. 5)

'Fear to stop & shame to fly'

In this design Blake succeeds in conveying a sense of uncertainty in the slightly absurd figures of his warriors hesitating which way to turn behind their fence of shields.

Design no. 92 (page 132, ms. no. 6)

The liberal Man inviting the traveller into his house

The last design of this series, surrounding a blank panel, clearly illustrates Blake's title but the subject does not seem to have any obvious relation to Gray's verses—unless it is meant to imply a welcome return to contemplation of the liberal arts at Cambridge in the next poem, after so many scenes of mindless violence. Or it could, perhaps, be related to the lines already illustrated in the second design, with their reference to Owen's 'liberal hand'.

ODE FOR MUSIC.
PERFORMED IN THE SENATE-HOUSE
AT CAMBRIDGE, JULY 1, 1769

Gray's 'Ode for Music' was composed in 1769 for the installation of the Duke of Grafton as Chancellor of the University of Cambridge. Blake betrays the fact that he had never been in Cambridge by his portrayal of the river Cam and the Backs of the Colleges in the fifth design, with an elaborate Gothic building in the background entirely unlike any building to be seen in the University.

Design no. 93 (page 133, ms. no. 1)

Fame

Surrounding the title-page of the 'Ode for Music' is a winged figure entitled 'Fame' by Blake, but equally well personifying Music with her trumpet. The night sky is sprinkled with stars, one shooting upwards, another fixed over the Seraph's head. Blake's idea of Cambridge has influenced his drawing of the University buildings at the foot of the painting. There are two more or less Gothic spires to represent the arts, but four other structures, one being a pyramid, are clearly 'mathematic forms', inspired by the thought of Newton, the scientific materialist, formerly in residence there.

65

Design no. 94 (page 134, ms. no. 2)

A bird singing

Surrounding the list of subjects for the Ode is a simple, yet attractive, drawing of 'A bird singing'; in other words, Nature's music. It is a larger version of the tiny figure illustrating the line, 'The Attic warbler pours her throat', in the third design for 'Ode on the Spring'. The bird is seated on a tendril coiling up into the sky.

Design no. 95 (page 135, ms. no. 3)

A Genius driving away 'Comus & his midnight crew'

Gray's Ode begins with a reference to Milton:

'Hence, avaunt, ('tis holy ground)

'Comus, and his midnight-crew. . .'

In Blake's design 'A Genius' with flashes of lightning on either side is driving away the 'midnight-crew'. Servitude is drawn as an evil figure trailing a heavy chain; her legs are coalescing to form a devil's tail. This can be paralleled by a drawing of a figure, 'half woman, half spectre' in *The Four Zoas*, Night 1, page 7. Flattery has painted cheeks and a hand turned into a serpent's head. Sloth is pale with staring eyes. Ignorance has a stupid face, though trying to look wise.

Design no. 96 (page 136, ms. no. 4)

Milton struck the corded shell

Newtons self bends from his state sublime

In the fourth illustration Milton is seen seated with his 'deep-ton'd shell' (though altered to 'corded shell' in Blake's caption). Beside him are growing a lily, the flower of innocence, and a sunflower, symbol of Man's aspirations. Looking down on him from a cloud is 'Meek Newton's self'. Milton with his stringed instrument, is naturally given a poetic beauty. Newton is also endowed with great nobility, as in other drawings of him by Blake, in spite of his having only the 'single vision' of an arch-materialist. Blake certainly admired his intellect and concentration even with their limitations and considered him a great artist in his way.

Design no. 97 (page 137, ms. no. 5)

'I wood the gleam of Cynthia silver bright

Where willowy Camus lingers with delight'

In this design Blake illustrates two lines of the poem, taking them out of order. He pictures a scene at the Backs of the Colleges where the poet meditates on the bank of the placid river Cam. Gray's lines,

'Ye brown o'er-arching Groves,

'That Contemplation loves,'

are represented by leafless trees on either side, contrasting with a bank of lively green foliage behind him. In the background is a Gothic spire with a crescent moon in the sky.

Design no. 98 (page 138, ms. no. 6)
>'*Great Edward with the lillies on his brow*
>*To hail the festal morning come*'

Blake again illustrates two non-consecutive lines which are widely separated in Gray's text. Gray explains in his note that it was Edward III who added the fleur de lys of France to the arms of England and founded Trinity College. In Blake's splendid vision King Edward is not only wearing the lilies on his head, but is also scattering them from both hands. He is accompanied by Margaret of Anjou on his left and on his right by a bearded man, crowned with laurel and carrying the Holy Bible, perhaps 'the murder'd Saint', King Henry VI, husband of Margaret and part-founder of Trinity College.

Design no. 99 (page 139, ms. no. 7)
>'*Leaning from her golden cloud*
>*The venerable Margaret*'

This design is a simple illustration of the poet's lines. Gray explains in his notes that 'the venerable Marg'ret' is the Countess of Richmond and Derby, mother of Henry VII and foundress of St. John's and Christ's Colleges. From her cloud she welcomes, though with admonishing finger, a black-gowned young man to the University.

Design no. 100 (page 140, ms. no. 8)
>'*The Laureate wreath*'

Gray again gives an explanation that 'the laureate wreath, that Cecil wore' refers to Lord Treasurer Burleigh, Chancellor of the University in the reign of Queen Elizabeth. Blake follows Gray in representing Cambridge by the tall figure of Granta, who is placing the wreath on the Duke of Grafton's head, so recognizing him as the new Chancellor.

Design no. 101 (page 141, ms. no. 9)
>'*Nor fear the rocks nor seek the shore*'

For this design Blake depicts the new Chancellor seated in the Ship of State, his hand on the tiller, his sail set and pennant flying in the wind. Below the pennant the Hanoverian 'star of Brunswick smiles serene'.

Design no. 102 (page 142, ms. no. 10)
>*Fame*

The painting, again entitled 'Fame' by Blake, shews a Seraph blowing a trumpet and carried up by huge, many-plumed wings. Her tunic is decorated by roughly sketched figures dancing in triumph with raised arms holding tambourines aloft.

EPITAPH ON MRS. CLARKE

Blake has written his titles for the two subjects of this short piece on the verso of the last leaf of the 'Ode for Music'. He has omitted the title-leaf for the 'Epitaph'.

Design no. 103 (page 145, ms. no. [1])

The mourner at the tomb

This design, executed entirely in black and grey washes, seems to convey only the general idea of Grief beside a tomb. His figure of Grief depicts the qualities of the dead woman, described in the poem, rather than any surviving mourners.

Design no. 104 (page 146, ms. no. [2])

Her infant image here below
Sits smiling on a Fathers woe

Blake shews the sorrowing father at his fireside, comforted by the mother's image surviving in her smiling daughter. It is difficult to interpret the meaning of the statue and two obelisks sketched on the panel above the fireplace, unless they be meant to draw attention to the uselessness of the conventional paraphernalia of mourning such as these monuments. They may even be Blake's method of teasing Flaxman about his professional preoccupation with this kind of sculpture.

ELEGY WRITTEN IN A COUNTRY CHURCH-YARD

It is a misfortune that the Elegy, universally accepted as Gray's best poem—classed, indeed, by some authorities as the greatest poem of the eighteenth century—should have come at the end of the volume. It was most probably begun in 1742, the impulse for its composition being the premature death of Gray's friend, Richard West. He worked at the poem at intervals in later years and sent it to Horace Walpole in its completed form in 1750. The position of the Elegy in the volume does not, therefore, represent its place in Gray's life, and it comes in the sequence at the end when Blake's powers of pictorial invention may have been flagging, so that Gray's greatest poem is not accompanied by Blake's finest designs. In addition, it is likely that Blake did not agree with Gray's exaggerated grief at the passage of a human being from vegetative life on earth to the better life of the spirit, nor did he altogether respect Gray's reverence for the Church, of whose oppressive effect on the life of the English countryside Blake was aware.

Design no. 105 (page 147, ms. no. 1)

The author writing

In the design surrounding the title-page, Blake has imagined the author working, not in the church-yard, but inside the church. He appears to suggest that the influence of the place might be too great by depicting the poet with his cloak thrown over his head as if to protect himself from the power of the three-decker pulpit with its purple hangings seen beyond the pillars on the right.

Design no. 106 (page 148, ms. no. 2)

Contemplation among Tombs

In the second illustration surrounding the list of his captions, Blake again shews the poet, with left foot advanced (symbolic of materialistic thought), standing beneath a tree, symbol of the vegetative life. At his side is the fine sculptured tomb of a knight contrasted with the plain grass-grown mound, bound with briars, covering the remains of one of the 'rude Forefathers of the hamlet'. This is shewn as a familiar Blake 'property', first seen in plate 44 of *Songs of Experience*, 1794, illustrating the lines in 'The Garden of Love':

> And Priests in black gowns, were walking their rounds,
> And binding with briars, my joys & desires.

The artist is thus drawing attention both to the social injustice of the peasant's lying uncommemorated side by side with the rich man's sepulchral splendour and to the falsity of the poet's grief. The latter idea was emphasized about the same time by Blake's engraving made in 1797 in the volume of Young's *Night Thoughts*, page 15, where the poet himself is bound with briars, emblematic of grief for his friend.

Design no. 107 (page 149, ms. no. 3)

> *'The Plowman homeward plods his weary way*
> *And leaves the world to Darkness & to me'*

Darkness, clothed in a habit resembling that of a nun, is seen descending over the poet. In the background is the imposing church in whose tower the curfew bell is ringing. Plodding past the poet are the plowman and his horse, both expressing utter weariness.

Design no. 108 (page 150, ms. no. 4)

> *'For him no more the blazing hearth shall burn*
> *Nor children run to lisp their sires return'*

In his illustration the widow and three children in black robes are mourning at the edge of the grave, the sexton is filling in the grave with his spade, while a prosperous, rather too elegant, clergyman is intoning the words of the burial service. Here there is a marked contrast between the hard lot of the peasant and the comfortable parson.

Design no. 109 (page 151, ms. no. 5)

> *'Oft did the Harvest to their sickle yield'*

Blake depicts a splendid countryman, combining in his appearance physical power with strength of character. Here, as elsewhere, he seems to be at pains to shew the superiority of the 'peasant' and producer over the other classes who feed upon his labour. The reaper is attended by a demure maiden carrying a small keg of beer.

Design no. 110 (page 152, ms. no. 6)

> *'Chill penury repressd their noble rage'*

In this design Blake drives further home the point of the peasant's hard life by drawing again another fine physical type digging the ground. The rather haggard small boy watching his father seems to embody their sufferings.

69

Design no. 111 (page 153, ms. no. 7)

'Some Village Hampden that with dauntless breast
The little Tyrant of his Fields withstood'

Here the peasant, spade in hand, with his cottage in the background, defies the mean-looking bailiff displaying his document legalized by a seal.

Design no. 112 (page 154, ms. no. 8)

'Many a holy text around she strews'

In this design one tombstone has collapsed, while on another, still upright, Gray's 'unletter'd Muse' is tracing the words:

DUST THOU ART
HERE LIETH
Wm Blake

with his age indistinctly added. It seems, however, to comprise three or four figures, as if shewing his belief that later ages would grant him fame and recognition.

Design no. 113 (page 155, ms. no. 9)

'Some kindred spirit shall inquire thy fate
Haply some hoary headed swain may say
Oft &c'

In the ninth design the poet has returned to the grass-grown mound bound with briars. He stands beside it, again with his left foot advanced, and is listening, book in hand, to 'some hoary headed swain' telling his memories of the dead man.

Design no. 114 (page 156, ms. no. 10)

'Slow thro the Churchway path we saw him borne'

The tenth design has some resemblance to the illustration for 'The Ecchoing Green' in *Songs of Innocence*, 1789, plate 6. It has the same quiet charm, with village women and their children seated beneath a protecting tree, though it is a less joyful scene that they are witnessing. One child is feeding at its mother's breast, another is holding out a ball to a woman beside him as a plaything.

Design no. 115 (page 157, ms. no. 11)

A Shepherd reading the Epitaph

The final illustration to the 'Elegy' is an empty and unimaginative scene. A shepherd is standing on the slab of a high tomb leaning on his staff while reading the Epitaph written by Gray for his friend.

Design no. 116 (page 158, ms. no. 12)

A Spirit conducted to Paradise

The probable meaning of this last design shewing one spirit conducting another to a higher realm has already been discussed in the Introduction. The design surrounds Blake's verses addressed to Mrs. Ann Flaxman.

Note on Portraits of Blake and Gray

Inserted at the beginning of the volume is a pencil drawing of Blake's head and shoulders in profile by John Flaxman, a life-like image of the artist in middle age.

Blake depicted Gray as 'the Author' several times in the course of illustrating his poems. The most successful attempt is in the first design after the title-page. In this he has caught a good likeness of the poet, based, it is plain, on the portrait painted by Ecchardt in 1747 and now in the National Portrait Gallery. Another good likeness is seen in the first illustration to 'The Progress of Poesy'. The image of the poet writing the 'Elegy', however, makes no attempt to get a likeness, and it is, in fact, a rather poor drawing. Later in life, probably about 1819, when he was making his so-called 'Visionary Heads' for John Varley, he made a rapid impression of Gray's profile. This catches admirably in a few lines the essence of William Mason's portrait of Gray, an image no doubt seen by Blake as the engraving published with the *Memoir* added to his edition of Gray's writings published in 1775. Blake's drawing, reproduced in the Blake Trust facsimile of the Gray designs, is now in Pembroke College, Cambridge, where Gray lived from 1756 until his death in 1771.

WILLIAM BLAKE

1757 Born 28 November at 28 Broad Street, Golden Square, London, the second child of James and Catherine Blake.

1767 Put to Pars's drawing school in the Strand. His brother Robert born.

1772 Apprenticed 4 August to James Basire, engraver, Great Queen Street, Lincoln's Inn Fields.

1779 His apprenticeship completed.

1780 Exhibited a water-colour drawing at the Royal Academy for the first time.

1782 Married Catherine Boucher, 18 August, and went to live at 23 Green Street, Leicester Fields.

1783 *Poetical Sketches* published.

1784 Moved to 27 Broad Street, Golden Square, and joined by Robert Blake.
Partnership with James Parker as print-sellers bgeun.

1787 Robert Blake died, February, aged 19.
Partnership with Parker dissolved.
Moved to 28 Poland Street.

1788 Plates of *There is No Natural Religion* and of *All Religions are One* etched.

1789 *Songs of Innocence* and *The Book of Thel* completed.

1790 *The Marriage of Heaven and Hell* begun.

1791 Moved to 13 Hercules Buildings, Lambeth. The first part of *The French Revolution* printed and abandoned.

1793 Completed *For Children: The Gates of Paradise, The Marriage of Heaven and Hell, Visions of the Daughters of Albion, America: A Prophecy.*

1794 Completed *Songs of Innocence and of Experience, The First Book of Urizen, Europe: A Prophecy.*

1795 Completed *The Song of Los, The Book of Ahania, The Book of Los.*

1796 *Vala, or The Four Zoas* begun.
Designs for Young's *Night Thoughts* begun.

1797 Engravings for Young's *Night Thoughts* published.

1797 Water-colour designs for Gray's *Poems* probably begun, commissioned by Flaxman.

1800 Moved, September, to Felpham, near Bognor, Sussex, under Hayley's patronage. *Little Tom the Sailor* published.

1802 Hayley's *Ballads* with Blake's engravings published in quarto.

1803 Quarrel, August, with Trooper Scofield of the Royal Dragoons.
Returned, September, to London to live at 17 South Molton Street.

1804 Tried for sedition 11 January at Chichester Assizes and acquitted.
The plates for *Milton* and *Jerusalem* begun.

1805 Hayley's *Ballads* with Blake's engravings published in octavo.
Blair's *Grave* published with Blake's designs engraved by Schiavonetti.

1808 *Milton* completed.

1809 'The Canterbury Pilgrims' painted in 'frescoe'.
A Descriptive Catalogue printed.
Exhibition of pictures opened at 28 Broad Street.

1810-16 Blake's life passed in obscurity.

1817 Introduced to John Linnell.

1818 *Jerusalem* completed.
For the Sexes: The Gates of Paradise published.
The Laocoön plate engraved.

1821 *On Homer, and On Virgil* etched.
Moved to 3 Fountain Court, Strand.
The wood engravings for Thornton's *Pastorals of Virgil* executed.

1822 *The Ghost of Abel* etched.

1825 Engravings for *Illustrations of the Book of Job* published.
Designs for Dante's *Inferno* begun.

1827 Seven plates for Dante's *Inferno* engraved.
Died at Fountain Court, 12 August. Buried in Bunhill Fields cemetery, 17 August.

1831 Mrs Blake died, 13 October.

72

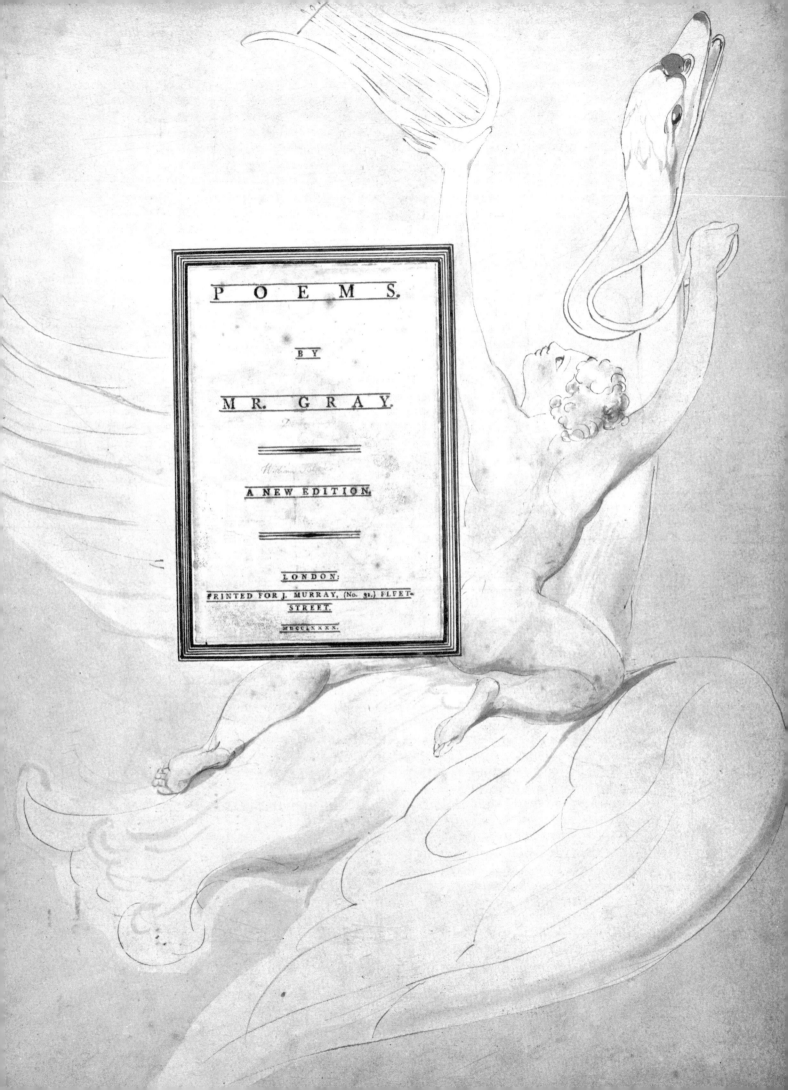

POEMS.

BY

MR. GRAY.

A NEW EDITION.

LONDON:
PRINTED FOR J. MURRAY, (No. 32.) FLEET-
STREET.
MDCCLXXXX.

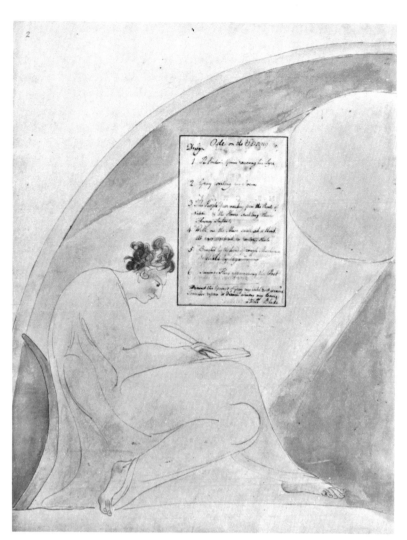

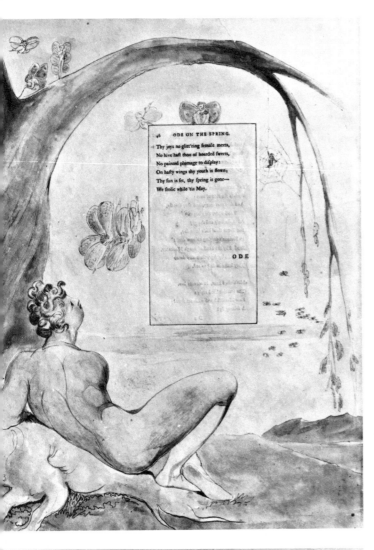

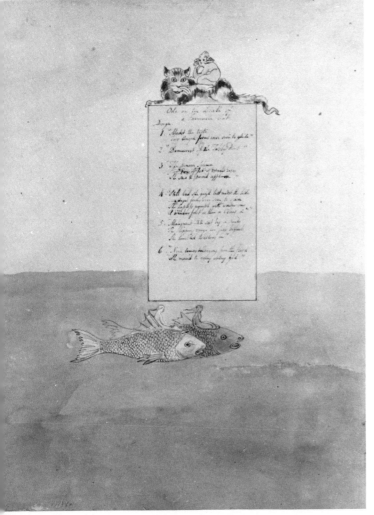

32   ODE ON THE DEATH

Her coat, that with the tortoise vies,
  Her ears of jet, and emerald eyes,
    She saw; and purr'd applause.

Still had she gaz'd; but 'midst the tide
Two angel forms were seen to glide,
  The Genii of the stream:
Their scaly armour's Tyrian hue,
Thro' richest purple to the view
  Betray'd a golden gleam.

The hapless nymph with wonder saw:
A whisker first, and then a claw,
  With many an ardent wish,
She stretch'd, in vain, to reach the prize.
What female heart can gold despise?
  What cat's averse to fish?

                              Presump-

OF A FAVOURITE CAT.   33

Presumptuous maid! with looks intent
Again she stretch'd, again she bent,
  Nor knew the gulph between:
(Malignant Fate sat by, and smil'd)
The slipp'ry verge her feet beguil'd,
  She tumbled headlong in.

Eight times emerging from the flood
She mew'd to ev'ry wat'ry God,
  Some speedy aid to send.
No Dolphin came, no Nereid stirr'd,
Nor cruel Tom, nor Susan heard,
  A fav'rite has no friend!

From hence, ye beauties, undeceiv'd,
Know, one false step is ne'er retriev'd,
  And be with caution bold.

                              Not

32   ODE, &c.

Nor all that tempts your wand'ring eyes,
And heedless hearts, is lawful prize;
  Nor all that glisters, gold.

                              ODE

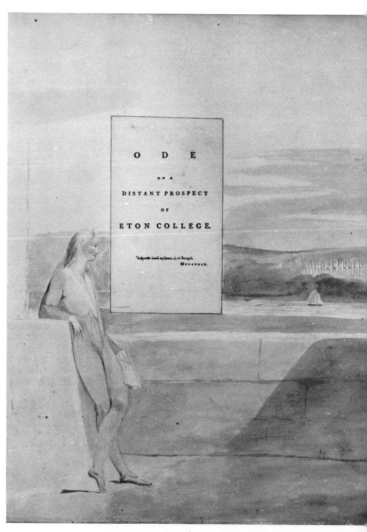

ODE

ON A

DISTANT PROSPECT

OF

ETON COLLEGE.

Ἄνθρωπος· ἱκανὴ πρόφασις εἰς τὸ δυστυχεῖν.
                              MENANDER.

ODE

ON A DISTANT PROSPECT OF

ETON COLLEGE.

YE distant spires, ye antique towers,
    That crown the wat'ry glade,
Where grateful Science still adores
    Her HENRY's holy shade;
And ye, that from the stately brow
Of WINDSOR's heights th' expanse below
Of grove, of lawn, of mead survey,
Whose turf, whose shade, whose flowers among
Wanders the hoary Thames along
    His silver-winding way.

Ah

36 ODE ON A DISTANT PROSPECT

Ah happy hills! ah pleasing shade!
Ah fields belov'd in vain!
Where once my careless childhood stray'd,
    A stranger yet to pain!
I feel, the gales that from ye blow,
A momentary bliss bestow,
As waving fresh their gladsome wing,
My weary soul they seem to sooth,
And, redolent of joy and youth,
    To breathe a second spring.

Say, Father THAMES, for thou hast seen
Full many a sprightly race
Disporting on thy margent green
The paths of pleasure trace,
Who foremost now delight to cleave,
With pliant arms, thy glassy wave?

The

OF ETON COLLEGE. 37

The captive linnet, which enthral?
What idle progeny succeed
To chase the rolling circle's speed,
    Or urge the flying ball?

While some on earnest business bent
Their murm'ring labours ply
'Gainst graver hours, that bring constraint
To sweeten liberty;
Some bold adventurers disdain
The limits of their little reign,
And unknown regions dare descry;
Still as they run they look behind,
They hear a voice in every wind,
    And snatch a fearful joy.

Gay hope is theirs by fancy fed,
Less pleasing when possest;
The tear forgot as soon as shed,
The sunshine of the breast:

Their

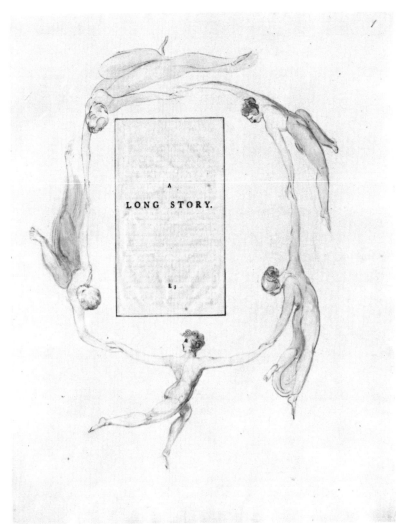

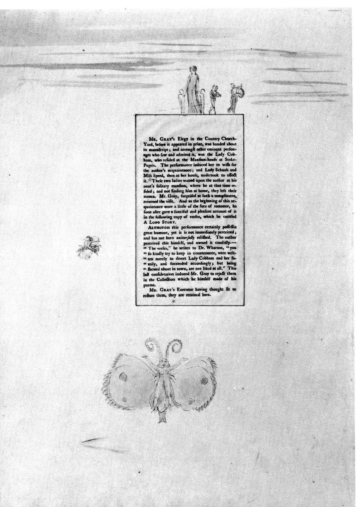

Mr. Gray's Elegy in the Country Church-
Yard, before it appeared in print, was handed about
in manuscript; and amongst other eminent person-
ages who saw and admired it, was the Lady Cobham, who resided at the Mansion-house at Stoke-
Pogeis. The performance induced her to wish for
the author's acquaintance; and Lady Schaub and
Miss Speed, then at her house, undertook to effect
it. These two ladies waited upon the author at his
aunt's solitary mansion, where he at that time resided; and not finding him at home, they left their
names. Mr. Gray, surprised at such a compliment,
returned the visit. And as the beginning of this acquaintance wore a little of the face of romance, he
soon after gave a fanciful and pleasant account of it
in following copy of verses, which he entitled
A Long Story.

Although this performance certainly possesses
great humour, yet it is not immediately perceived;
and has not been universally relished. The author
perceived this himself, and owned it candidly.—
"The verses," he writes to Dr. Wharton, "you
"so kindly try to keep in countenance, were wri-
"ten merely to divert Lady Cobham and her fa-
"mily, and succeeded accordingly; but being
"shewed about in town, are not liked at all." This
half consideration induced Mr. Gray to reject them
in the Collection which he himself made of his
poems.

Mr. Gray's Executor having thought fit to
restore them, they are retained here.

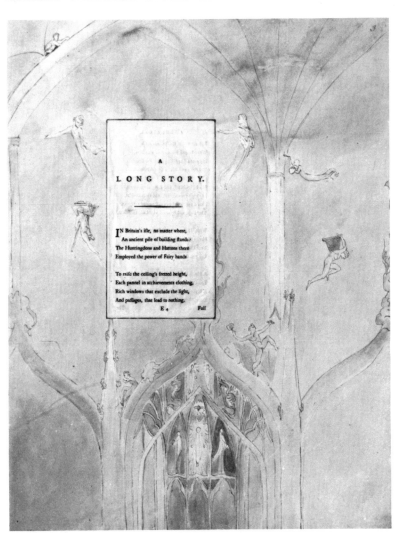

A

LONG STORY.

———

IN Britain's isle, no matter where,
An ancient pile of building stands:
The Huntingdon and Hatton there
Employed the power of Fairy hands

To raise the ceiling's fretted height,
Each pannel in atchievements clothing,
Rich windows that exclude the light,
And passages, that lead to nothing.

E 4   Full

Full oft within the spacious walls,
When he had fifty winters o'er him,
My grave Lord-Keeper led the Brawls;
The Seals and Maces danc'd before him.

His bushy beard, and shoe-strings green,
His high-crown'd hat, and satin doublet,
Mov'd the stout heart of England's Queen,
Tho' Pope and Spaniard could not trouble it.

What, in the very first beginning!
Shame of the versifying tribe!
Your Hist'ry whither are you spinning?
Can you do nothing but describe?

A House there is, (and that's enough)
From whence one fatal morning issues
A brace of warriors, not in buff,
But rustling in their silks and tissues.

The

The first came cap-a-pee from France
Her conqu'ring destiny fulfilling,
Whom meaner beauties eye askance,
And vainly ape her art of killing.

The other Amazon kind heaven
Had arm'd with spirit, wit, and satire:
But Cobham had the polish given,
And tipp'd her arrows with good-nature.

To celebrate her eyes, her hair—
Coarse panegyrics would but teaze her,
Melissa is her Nom de Guerre.
Alas, who would not wish to please her!

With bonnet blue and capuchin,
And aprons long they hid their armour,
And veil'd their weapons bright and keen
In pity to the country-farmer.

Fame

Fame in the shape of Mr. P—tt
(By this time all the parish know it)
Had told, that thereabouts there lurk'd
A wicked Imp they call a Poet:

Who prowl'd the country far and near,
Bewitch'd the children of the peasants,
Dried up the cows, and lam'd the deer,
And suck'd the eggs, and kill'd the pheasants.

My Lady heard their joint petition,
Swore by her coronet and ermine,
She'd issue out her high commission
To rid the manor of such vermin.

The Heroines undertook the task,
Thro' lanes unknown, o'er stiles they ventur'd,
Rapp'd at the door, nor stay'd to ask,
But bounce into the parlour enter'd.

The

The trembling family they daunt,
They flirt, they sing, they laugh, they tattle,
Rummage his Mother, pinch his Aunt,
And up stairs in a whirlwind rattle.

Each hole and cupboard they explore,
Each crook and cranny of his chamber,
Run hurry-skurry round the floor,
And o'er the bed and tester clamber;

Into the Drawers and China pry,
Papers and books, a huge Imbroglio!
Under a tea cup he might lie,
Or creased like dog-ears, in a folio.

On the first marching of the troops
The Muses, hopeless of his pardon,
Convey'd him underneath their hoops,
To a small closet in the garden.

So

So Rumour says: (Who will, believe.)
But that they left the door a-jar,
Where, safe and laughing in his sleeve,
He heard the distant din of war.

Short was his joy. He little knew
The power of magic was no fable;
Out of the window, whisk, they flew,
But left a spell upon the table.

The words too eager to unriddle
The poet felt a strange disorder:
Transparent birdlime form'd the middle,
And chains invisible the border,

So cunning was the Apparatus,
The powerful pothooks did so move him,
That, will he, nill he, to the Great-house
He went, as if the devil drove him.
  Yet

Yet on his way (no sign of grace,
For folks in fear are apt to pray)
To Phœbus he preferr'd his case,
And begg'd his aid that dreadful day.

The Godhead would have back'd his quarrel,
But with a blush on recollection
Own'd that his quiver and his laurel
'Gainst four such eyes were no protection.

The Court was sat, the Culprit there,
Forth from their gloomy mansions creeping
The Lady Janes and Joans repair,
And from the gallery stand peeping:

Such as in silence of the night
Come (sweep) along some winding entry
(Styack has often seen the sight)
Or at the chapel-door stand sentry;
  In

In peaked hoods and mantles tarnish'd,
Sour visages, enough to scare ye,
High Dames of honour once, that garnish'd
The drawing-room of fierce Queen Mary!

The Peeress comes. The Audience stare,
And doff their hats with due submission:
She curtsies, as she takes her chair,
To all the People of condition.

The Bard with many an artful fib,
Had in imagination fenc'd him,
Disprov'd the arguments of Squib,
And all that Groom could urge against him;

But soon his rhetoric forsook him,
When he the solemn hall had seen;
A sudden fit of ague shook him,
He stood as mute as poor Macleane.
  Yet

Yet something he was heard to mutter,
'How in the Park beneath an old tree,
'(Without design to hurt the butter,
'Or any malice to the poultry,)

'He once or twice had penn'd a sonnet;
'Yet hop'd that he might save his bacon:
'Numbers would give their oaths upon it,
'He ne'er was for a conj'rer taken.'

The ghostly prudes with hagged face
Already had condemn'd the sinner,
My Lady rose, and with a grace—
She smil'd, and bid him come to dinner.

'Jesu-Maria! Madam Bridget,
'Why what can the Viscountess mean?'
(Cried the square Hoods in woeful fidget)
'The times are alter'd quite and clean:
  Decorum's

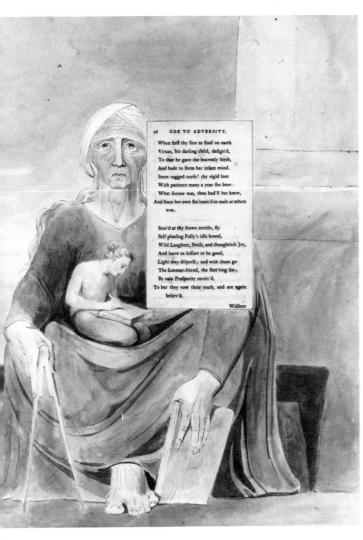

When first thy Sire to fend on earth
Virtue, his darling child, defign'd,
To thee he gave the heavenly birth,
And bade to form her infant mind.
Stern rugged nurfe! thy rigid lore
With patience many a year fhe bore:
What forrow was, thou bad'ft her know,
And from her own fhe learn'd to melt at others
woe.

Scar'd at thy frown terrific, fly
Self-pleafing Folly's idle brood,
Wild Laughter, Noife, and thoughtlefs Joy,
And leave us leifure to be good,
Light they difperfe; and with them go
The fummer-friend, the flatt'ring foe;
By vain Profperity receiv'd,
To her they vow their truth, and are again
believ'd.

Wifdom

Wifdom in fable garb array'd,
Immers'd in rapt'rous thought profound,
And Melancholy, filent maid
With leaden eye, that loves the ground,
Still, on thy folemn fteps attend:
Warm Charity, the general friend,
With Justice to herfelf fevere,
And Pity, dropping foft the fadly-pleafing tear.

Oh, gently on thy fuppliant's head,
Dread Goddefs, lay thy chaft'ning hand!
Not in the Gorgon terrors clad,
(As by the impious thou art feen)
With thund'ring voice, and threat'ning mien,
With fcreaming Horror's funeral cry,
Defpair, and fell Difeafe, and ghaftly Poverty.

F 3   Thy

Thy form benign, oh Goddefs, wear,
Thy milder influence impart,
Thy philofophic train be there
To foften, not to wound my heart.
The gen'rous fpark extinct revive,
Teach me to love, and to forgive,
Exact my own defects to fcan,
What others are to feel, and know myfelf a
man.

THE

THE

PROGRESS of POESY.

A

PINDARIC ODE.

Φωνᾶντα συνετοῖσι· ἐς
δὲ τὸ πᾶν ἑρμανέων
χατίζει. ————
        PINDAR, Olymp. II.

F 4

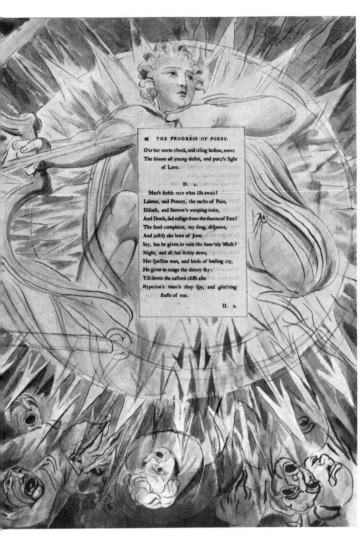

O'er her warm cheek, and rising bosom, move
The bloom of young desire, and purple light
of Love.

II. 1.

Man's feeble race what ills await!
Labour, and Penury, the racks of Pain,
Disease, and Sorrow's weeping train,
And Death, sad refuge from the storms of Fate!
The fond complaint, my song, disprove,
And justify the laws of Jove.
Say, has he given in vain the heav'nly Muse?
Night, and all her sickly dews,
Her spectres wan, and birds of boding cry,
He gives to range the dreary sky:
Till down the eastern cliffs afar
Hyperion's march they spy, and glitt'ring
shafts of war.

II. 2.

II. 2.

In climes beyond the solar road,
Where shaggy forms o'er ice-built mountains
roam,
The Muse has broke the twilight-gloom,
To cheer the shiv'ring native's dull abode.
And oft beneath the od'rous shade
Of Chili's boundless forests laid,
She deigns to hear the savage youth repeat
In loose numbers wildly sweet
Their feather-cinctur'd chiefs, and dusky loves.
Her track, where'er the Goddess roves,
Glory pursue, and gen'rous Shame,
Th' unconquerable mind, and Freedom's holy
flame.

II. 3.

Woods that wave o'er Delphi's steep,
Isles, that crown th' Ægean deep,

Fields,

Fields, that cool Ilissus laves,
Or where Mæander's amber waves
In lingering lab'rinths creep,
How do your tuneful echoes languish,
Mute, but to the voice of Anguish?
Where each old poetic mountain
Inspiration breath'd around:
Ev'ry shade and hallow'd fountain
Murmur'd deep a solemn sound:
Till the sad Nine, in Greece's evil hour,
Left their Parnassus for the Latian plains.
Alike they scorn the pomp of tyrant Power,
And coward Vice, that revels in her chains.
When Latium had her lofty spirit lost,
They sought, oh Albion! next thy sea-en-
circled coast.

III. 1.

III. 1.

Far from the sun and summer-gale,
In thy green lap was Nature's darling laid,
What time, where lucid Avon stray'd,
To him the mighty mother did unveil
Her awful face: the dauntless child
Stretch'd forth his little arms, and smil'd.
This pencil take (she said) whose colours clear
Richly paint the vernal year:
Thine too these golden keys, immortal boy!
This can unlock the gates of Joy;
Of Horror that, and thrilling Fears,
Or ope the sacred source of sympathetic Tears.

III. 2.

Nor second he, that rode sublime
Upon the seraph-wings of Ecstasy,
The secrets of th' abyss to spy.
He pass'd the flaming bounds of Place and Time:

The

THE PROGRESS OF POESY.

The living throne, the sapphire blaze,
Where angels tremble, while they gaze,
He saw; but, blasted with excess of light,
Clos'd his eyes in endless night.
Behold, where Dryden's less presumptuous car,
Wide o'er the fields of glory bear
Two coursers of ethereal race,
With necks in thunder cloth'd, and long-
resounding pace.

III. 3.

Hark, his hands the lyre explore!
Bright-eyed Fancy, hov'ring o'er,
Scatters from her pictur'd urn
Thoughts that breathe, and words that burn.
But ah! 'tis heard no more—
Oh! Lyre divine, what daring spirit
Wakes thee now? tho' he inherit

Nor

A PINDARIC ODE.

Nor the pride, nor ample pinion,
That the Theban Eagle bear,
Sailing with supreme dominion
Thro' the azure deep of air:
Yet oft before his infant eyes would run
Such forms as glitter in the Muse's ray,
With orient hues, unborrow'd of the sun:
Yet shall he mount, and keep his distant way
Beyond the limits of a vulgar fate,
Beneath the Good how far—but far above the
Great.

G   THE

The Bard.

1. A Welsh Bard.
2. The Slaughterd Bards taken from the line
3. The Bard escaping Edwards fate.
4.
5.
6. The gentle Cliffs. "I see them sit"
7.
8. The Weaving. "Weave in grim repose"
9.
10.
11.
12.
13.
14.

THE

B A R D.

A

PINDARIC ODE.

G 2

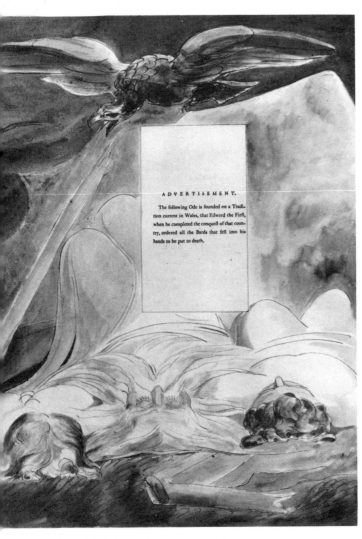

The following Ode is founded on a Tradi-
tion current in Wales, that Edward the First,
when he completed the conquest of that country, ordered all the Bards that fell into his
hands to be put to death.

THE

BARD.

A PINDARIC ODE.

I. 1.

'RUIN seize thee, ruthless King,
' Confusion on thy banners wait;
'Tho' fann'd by Conquest's crimson wing,
'They mock the air with idle state!
'Helm, nor Hauberk's twisted mail,
'Nor even thy virtues, Tyrant, shall avail

G 3   'To

96   THE BARD

' To save thy secret soul from nightly fears,
' From Cambria's curse, from Cambria's tears!'
Such were the sounds that o'er the crested pride
Of the first Edward scatter'd wild dismay,
As down the steep of Snowdon's shaggy side
He wound with toilsome march his long array.
Stout Glo'ster stood aghast in speechless trance!
To arms! cried Mortimer, and couch'd his
                quiv'ring lance.

I. 2.

On a rock, whose haughty brow
Frowns o'er old Conway's foaming flood,
Robed in the sable garb of woe,
With haggard eyes the Poet stood;
(Loose his beard, and hoary hair
Stream'd, like a meteor, to the troubled air;)
And with a master's hand, and prophet's fire,
Struck the deep sorrows of his lyre.

                                        'Hark.

A PINDARIC ODE.   97

'Hark, how each giant-oak, and desert-cave,
'Sigh to the torrent's awful voice beneath!
'O'er thee, oh King! their hundred arms
'   they wave,
'Revenge on thee in hoarser murmurs breathe;
'Vocal no more, since Cambria's fatal day,
'To high-born Hoel's harp, or soft Llewel-
'   lyn's lay.

I. 3.

'Cold is Cadwallo's tongue,
'That hush'd the stormy main:
'Brave Urien sleeps upon his craggy bed:
'Mountains, ye mourn in vain
'Modred, whose magic song
'Made huge Plinlimmon bow his cloud-top'd
'   head.

G 4   'On

'On dreary Arvon's shore they lie,
'Smear'd with gore, and ghastly pale:
'Far, far aloof th' affrighted ravens sail;
'The famish'd eagle screams, and passes by.
'Dear lost companions of my tuneful art,
'Dear, as the light that visits these sad eyes,
'Dear, as the ruddy drops that warm my heart,
'Ye died amidst your dying country's cries—
'No more I weep. They do not sleep.
'On yonder cliffs, a grisly band,
'I see them sit, they linger yet,
'Avengers of their native land:
'With me in dreadful harmony they join,
'And weave with bloody hands the tissue of
'thy line.'

II. 1.

'Weave the warp, and weave the woof,
'The winding-sheet of Edward's race.
'Give

'Give ample room, and verge enough
'The characters of hell to trace.
'Mark the year, and mark the night,
'When Severn shall re-echo with affright
'The shrieks of death, thro' Berkley's roofs
'that ring,
'Shrieks of an agonizing King!
'She-wolf of France, with unrelenting fangs,
'That tear'st the bowels of thy mangled mate,
'From thee be born, who o'er thy country
'hangs
'The scourge of Heav'n. What terrors
'round him wait!
'Amazement in his van, with flight combin'd,
'And Sorrow's faded form, and Solitude
'behind.

II. 2.

'Mighty Victor, mighty Lord,
'Low on his funeral couch he lies!
'No

'No pitying heart, no eye, afford
'A tear to grace his obsequies.
'Is the sable warrior fled?
'Thy son is gone. He rests among the dead.
'The swarm that in thy noon-tide beam were
'born?
'Gone to salute the rising Morn.   [blows,
'Fair laughs the Morn, and soft the zephyr
'While proudly riding o'er the azure realm
'In gallant trim the gilded vessel goes;
'Youth on the prow, and pleasure at the helm;
'Regardless of the sweeping Whirlwind's sway,
'That, hush'd in grim repose, expects his
'evening-prey.

II. 3.

'Fill high the sparkling bowl,
'The rich repast prepare,
'Reft of a crown, he yet may share the feast:
'Close by the regal chair

'Fell thirst and famine scowl
'A baleful smile upon their baffled guest.
'Heard ye the din of battle bray,
'Lance to lance, and horse to horse?
'Long years of havoc urge their destin'd course,
'And thro' the kindred squadrons mow their
'way.
'Ye towers of Julius, London's lasting shame,
'With many a foul and midnight murder fed,
'Revere his consort's faith, his father's fame,
'And spare the meek usurper's holy head.
'Above, below, the rose of snow,
'Twin'd with her blushing foe, we spread:
'The bristled boar in infant gore
'Wallows beneath the thorny shade.
'Now, Brothers, bending o'er th' accursed
'loom
'Stamp we our vengeance deep, and ratify
'his doom.

III.

III. 1.

" Edward, lo! to sudden fate
" (Weave we the woof. The thread is spun,)
" Half of thy heart we consecrate.
" (The web is wove. The work is done.)"
" Stay, oh stay! nor thus forlorn,
" Leave me unbless'd, unpity'd, here to mourn:
" In yon bright track, that fires the western skies,
" They melt, they vanish from my eyes.
" But oh! what solemn scenes on Snowdon's
     " height
" Descending slow their glitt'ring skirts unroll?
" Visions of glory! spare my aching sight,
" Ye unborn ages, crowd not on my soul!
" No more our long-lost Arthur we bewail.
" All-hail, ye genuine Kings, Britannia's issue,
     " hail!

           III.

III. 2.

' Girt with many a Baron bold
' Sublime their starry fronts they rear;
' And gorgeous Dames, and Statesmen old
' In bearded majesty, appear.
' In the midst a form divine!
' Her eye proclaims her of the Briton-line;
' Her lion-port, her awe-commanding face,
' Attemper'd sweet to virgin-grace.
' What strings symphonious tremble in the air!
' What strains of vocal transport round her play!
' Hear from the grave, great Taliessin, hear;
' They breathe a soul to animate thy clay.
' Bright Rapture calls, and soaring, as she sings,
' Waves in the eye of Heaven her many-co-
     ' lour'd wings.

           III.

III. 3.

' The verse adorn again
' Fierce War, and faithful Love,
' And Truth severe, by fairy Fiction drest.
' In buskin'd measures move
' Pale Grief, and pleasing pain,
' With Horror, tyrant of the throbbing breast.
' A voice, as of the cherub-choir,
' Gales from blooming Eden bear;
' And distant warblings lessen on my ear,
' That lost in long futurity expire.
' Fond impious man, think'st thou yon san-
     ' guine cloud,
' Rais'd by thy breath, has quench'd the orb
     ' of day?
' To-morrow he repairs the golden flood,
' And warms the nations with redoubled ray.

           ' Enough

' Enough for me: with joy I see
' The different doom our fates assign.
' Be thine Despair, and scepter'd Care;
' To triumph, and to die, are mine.'
He spoke, and headlong, from the mountain's
     height,
Deep in the roaring tide he plung'd to endless
     night.

           THE

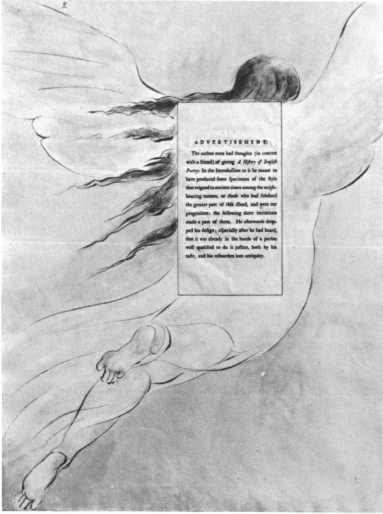

them, till looking through an opening in the
rocks, he saw twelve gigantic figures resembling women: they were all employed about
a loom, and as they wove, they sung the following dreadful song; which when they had
finished, they tore the web into twelve pieces,
and, each taking her portion, galloped six to
the north, and as many to the south.

THE

THE

FATAL SISTERS.

AN ODE.

NOW the storm begins to lour,
(Haste, the loom of hell prepare,)
Iron sleet of arrowy shower
Hurtles in the darkened air.

Glitt'ring lances are the loom,
Where the dusky warp we strain,
Weaving many a soldier's doom,
Orkney's woe, and Randver's bane.

H 3   See

See the grisly texture grow!
('Tis of human entrails made,)
And the weights that play below,
Each a gasping warrior's head.

Shafts for shuttles, dipt in gore,
Shoot the trembling cords along,
Sword, that once a monarch bore,
Keep the tissue close and strong.

Mista, black terrific maid,
Sangrida, and Hilda, see!
Join the wayward work to aid:
'Tis the woof of victory.

Ere the ruddy sun be set,
Pikes must shiver, javelins sing,
Blade with clatt'ring buckler meet,
Hauberk crash, and helmet ring.

(Weave

(Weave the crimson web of war.)
Let us go, and let us fly,
Where our friends the conflict share,
Where they triumph, where they die.

As the paths of fate we tread,
Wading thro' th' ensanguin'd field,
Gondula, and Geira, spread
O'er the youthful King your shield.

We the reins to slaughter give,
Ours to kill, and ours to spare:
Spite of danger he shall live.
(Weave the crimson web of war.)

They, whom once the desert-beach
Pent within its bleak domain,
Soon their ample sway shall stretch
O'er the plenty of the plain.

H 4   Low

114   THE FATAL SISTERS.

Low the dauntless Earl is laid,
Gor'd with many a gaping wound:
Fate demands a nobler head;
Soon a King shall bite the ground.

Long his loss shall Eirin weep,
Ne'er again his likeness see;
Long her strains in sorrow steep,
Strains of immortality!

Horror covers all the heath,
Clouds of carnage blot the sun.
Sisters, weave the web of death,
Sisters, cease: The work is done.

Hail the task, and hail the hands!
Songs of joy and triumph sing;
Joy to the victorious bands;
Triumph to the younger King.
                        Mortal,

AN ODE.   115

Mortal, thou that hear'st the tale,
Learn the tenour of our song.
Scotland, thro' each winding vale,
Far and wide the notes prolong.

Sisters, hence, with spurs of speed!
Each her thundering faulchion wield,
Each bestride her sable steed.
Hurry, hurry, to the field!
                        THE

THE
DESCENT OF ODIN.

AN ODE.

(From the Norse Tongue.)

To be found in Bartholinus, de causis
contemnendæ mortis; Hafniæ, 1689,
Quarto.

Uprais Odinn Alida gauta, &c.

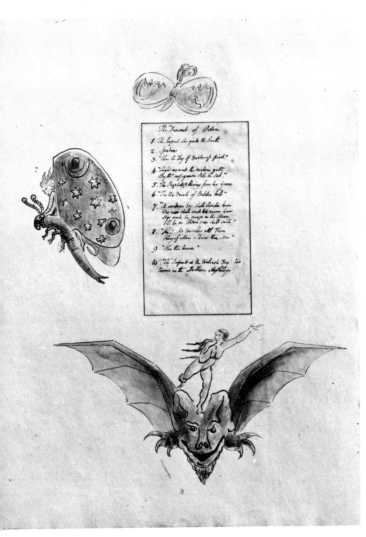

120   THE DESCENT OF ODIN.

PROPHETESS.

Mantling in the goblet see
The pure bev'rage of the bees,
O'er it hangs the shield of gold:
'Tis the drink of *Balder* bold.
Balder's head to death is giv'n.
Pain can reach the Sons of Heav'n!
Unwilling I my lips unclose:
Leave me, leave me to repose.

ODIN.

Once again my call obey,
Prophetess, arise, and say,
What dangers *Odin's* child await,
Who the author of his fate.

PROPHETESS.

In *Hoder's* hand the hero's doom;
His brother sends him to the tomb.

Now

AN ODE.   123

Now my weary lips I close:
Leave me, leave me to repose.

ODIN.

Prophetess, my spell obey:
Once again arise, and say,
Who th' avenger of his guilt,
By whom shall *Hoder's* blood be spilt.

PROPHETESS.

In the caverns of the west,
By *Odin's* fierce embrace comprest,
A wond'rous boy shall *Rinda* bear,
Who ne'er shall comb his raven hair,
Nor wash his visage in the stream,
Nor see the sun's departing beam,
Till he on *Hoder's* corse shall smile
Flaming on the funeral pile.
Now my weary lips I close:
Leave me, leave me to repose.

I   ODIN.

124   THE DESCENT OF ODIN.

ODIN.

Yet awhile my call obey;
Prophetess, awake, and say,
What Virgins these, in speechless woe,
That bend to earth their solemn brow,
That their flaxen tresses tear,
And snowy veils, that float in air.
Tell me whence their sorrows rose:
Then I leave thee to repose.

PROPHETESS.

Ha! no Traveller art thou,
King of Men, I know thee now;
Mightiest of a mighty line———

ODIN.

No boding Maid of skill divine
Art thou, nor Prophetess of good,
But mother of the giant-brood!

PRO.

AN ODE.   125

PROPHETESS.

Hie thee hence, and boast at home,
That never shall enquirer come
To break my iron-sleep again;
Till *Lok* has burst his tenfold chain.
Never, till substantial Night
Has reassum'd her ancient right;
Till wrapt in flames, in ruin hurl'd,
Sinks the fabric of the world.

I 2   THE

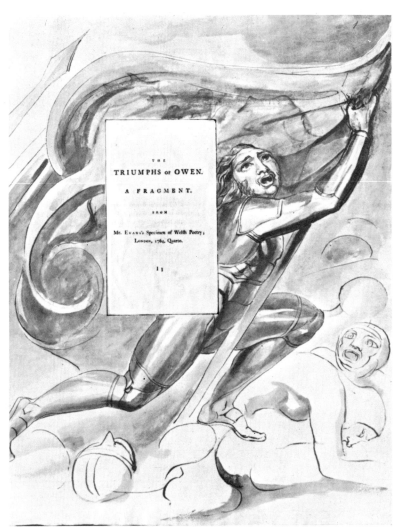

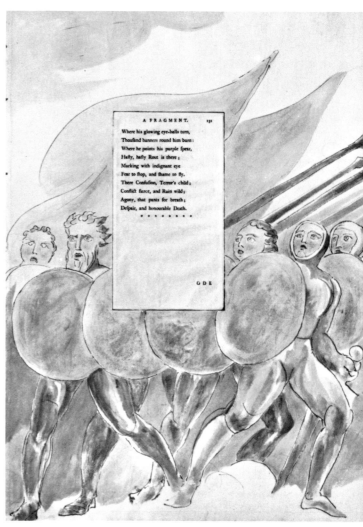

130   TRIUMPHS OF OWEN.

Big with hosts of mighty name,
Squadrons three against him came:
This the force of Eirin hiding;
Side by side as proudly riding,*
On her shadow long and gay
Lochlin plows the wat'ry way:
There the Norman sails afar
Catch the winds, and join the war:
Black and huge along they sweep,
Burthens of the angry deep.

Dauntless on his native sands
The dragon-son of Mona stands;
In glittering arms and glory dreft,
High he rears his ruby creft,
There the thund'ring ftrokes begin,
There the prefs, and there the din;
Talymalfra's rocky fhore
Echoing to the battle's roar.

                              Where

A FRAGMENT.   131

Where his glowing eye-balls turn,
Thousand banners round him burn;
Where he points his purple spear,
Hasty, hasty Rout is there;
Marking with indignant eye
Fear to stop, and shame to fly.
There Confusion, Terror's child;
Conflict fierce, and Ruin wild;
Agony, that pants for breath;
Despair, and honourable Death.
* * * * * * *

                              ODE

ODE FOR MUSIC.

PERFORMED IN THE

SENATE-HOUSE

AT

CAMBRIDGE, JULY 1, 1769,

At the INSTALLATION of his Grace
AUGUSTUS-HENRY FITZROY, Duke of
GRAFTON, Chancellor of the University.

136 ODE FOR MUSIC.

Great Edward, with the lilies on his brow
From haughty Gallia torn,
And sad Chatillon, on her bridal morn
That wept her bleeding Love, and princely
  Clare,
And Anjou's Heroine, and the paler Rose,
The rival of her crown and of her woes,
And either Henry there,
The murder'd Saint, and the majestic Lord,
That broke the bonds of Rome.
(Their tears, their little triumphs o'er,
Their human passions now no more,
Save Charity, that glows beyond the tomb)
All that on Granta's fruitful plain
Rich streams of regal bounty pour'd,
And bad these awful fanes and turrets rise,
To hail their Fitzroy's festal morning come;
And thus they speak in soft accord
The liquid language of the skies.

              V.

ODE FOR MUSIC. 137

V.

"What is grandeur, what is Power?
"Heavier toil, superior pain.
"What the bright reward we gain?
"The grateful memory of the Good.
"Sweet is the breath of vernal shower,
"The bee's collected treasures sweet,
"Sweet music's melting fall, but sweeter yet
"The still small voice of Gratitude."

VI.

Foremost and leaning from her golden cloud
The venerable Marg'ret see!
"Welcome, my noble Son, (she cries aloud)
"To this, thy kindred train, and me:
"Pleas'd in thy lineaments we trace
"A Tudor's fire, a Beaufort's grace,
"Thy liberal heart, thy judging eye,
"The flower unheeded shall descry,

K   "And

140 ODE FOR MUSIC.

"And bid it round heav'n's altars shed
"The fragrance of its blushing head:
"Shall raise from earth the latent gem
"To glitter on the diadem.

VII.

"Lo, Granta waits to lead her blooming band,
"Not obvious, not obtrusive, She
"No vulgar praise, no venal incense flings;
"Nor dares with courtly tongue refin'd
"Profane thy inborn royalty of mind:
"She revers herself and thee.
"With modest pride to grace thy youthful
  "brow
"The laureate wreath, that Cecil wore, she
  "brings,
"And to thy just, thy gentle hand
"Submits the Fasces of her sway,

         "While

ODE FOR MUSIC. 141

"While Spirits blest above and Men below
"Join with glad voice the loud symphonious
  "lay.

VIII.

"Thro' the wild waves as they roar
"With watchful eye and dauntless mien
"Thy steady course of honour keep,
"Nor fear the rocks, nor seek the shore:
"The star of Brunswick smiles serene,
"And gilds the horrors of the deep."

K 2   EPI.

EPITAPH
ON
MRS. CLARKE.

LO! where this silent marble weeps,
A Friend, a Wife, a Mother sleeps;
A Heart, within whose sacred cell
The peaceful Virtues lov'd to dwell.
Affection warm, and Faith sincere,
And soft Humanity were there.
In agony, in death resign'd,
She felt the wound she left behind.

116 EPITAPH, &c.

Her infant image, here below,
Sits smiling on a father's woe:
Whom what awaits, while yet he strays
Along the lonely vale of days?
A pang to secret sorrow dear;
A sigh; an unavailing tear;
Till time shall ev'ry grief remove,
With Life, with Memory, and with Love.

ELEGY.

ELEGY
WRITTEN IN A
COUNTRY CHURCH-YARD.

Can storied urn or animated bust,
Back to its mansion call the fleeting breath?
Can Honour's voice provoke the silent dust,
Or Flattery sooth the dull cold ear of Death?

Perhaps in this neglected spot is laid
Some heart once pregnant with celestial fire;
Hands that the rod of empire might have sway'd,
Or wak'd to ecstasy the living lyre.

But Knowledge to their eyes her ample page
Rich with the spoils of Time did ne'er unroll;
Chill Penury repress'd their noble rage,
And froze the genial current of the soul.

Full many a gem of purest ray serene,
The dark unfathom'd caves of Ocean bear:
Full many a flower is born to blush unseen,
And waste its sweetness on the desert air.

Some

Somevillage-Hampden, that with dauntless breast,
The little tyrant of his fields withstood,
Some mute inglorious Milton here may rest,
Some Cromwell guiltless of his country's blood.

Th' applause of list'ning senates to command,
The threats of pain and ruin to despise,
To scatter plenty o'er a smiling land,
And read their hist'ry in a nation's eyes,

Their lot forbade: nor circumscrib'd alone
Their growing virtues, but their crimes confin'd;
Forbade to wade thro' slaughter to a throne,
And shut the gates of mercy on mankind.

The struggling pangs of conscious Truth to hide,
To quench the blushes of ingenuous Shame,
Or heap the shrine of Luxury and Pride
With incense kindled at the Muses flame.

Far

Far from the madding crowd's ignoble strife,
Their sober wishes never learn'd to stray;
Along the cool sequester'd vale of life
They kept the noiseless tenour of their way.

Yet ev'n these bones from insult to protect,
Some frail memorial still erected nigh,
With uncouth rhymes and shapeless sculpture deck'd,
Implores the passing tribute of a sigh.

Their name, their years, spelt by th' unletter'd
The place of fame and elegy supply: [Muse,
And many a holy text around she strews,
That teach the rustic moralist to die.

For who, to dumb Forgetfulness a prey,
This pleasing anxious being e'er resign'd,
Left the warm precincts of the chearful day,
Nor cast one longing ling'ring look behind?

On

On some fond breast the parting soul relies,
Some pious drops the closing eye requires;
Ev'n from the tomb the voice of Nature cries,
Ev'n in our ashes live their wonted fires.

For thee, who mindful of th' unhonour'd Dead
Dost in these lines their artless tale relate;
If chance, by lonely Contemplation led,
Some kindred spirit shall inquire thy fate,

Haply some hoary-headed swain may say,
'Oft have we seen him at the peep of dawn,
'Brushing with hasty steps the dews away,
'To meet the sun upon the upland lawn.

'There at the foot of yonder nodding beech,
'That wreathes its old fantastic roots so high,
'His listless length at noon-tide would he stretch,
'And pore upon the brook that babbles by.

L   'Hard

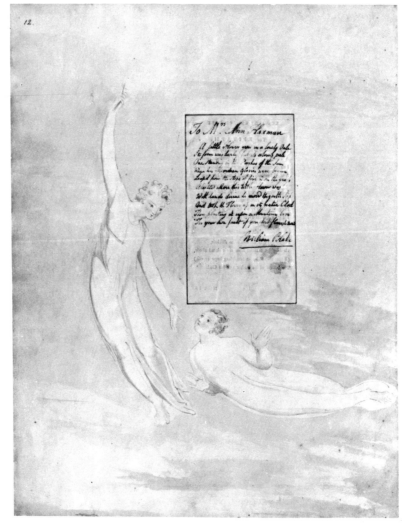